I0043045

Delphi Programming Essentials

Definitive Reference for Developers and Engineers

Richard Johnson

© 2025 by **NOBTREX** LLC. All rights reserved.

This publication may not be reproduced, distributed, or transmitted in any form or by any means, electronic or mechanical, without written permission from the publisher. Exceptions may apply for brief excerpts in reviews or academic critique.

Contents

Introduction

This book, *Delphi Programming Essentials*, provides an in-depth and comprehensive exploration of the Delphi programming language and its ecosystem. It is designed as a definitive guide for developers who seek to deepen their understanding of Delphi's core principles, advanced features, and practical application in modern software development. Emphasizing professional rigor and clarity, this work systematically covers fundamental to advanced topics that collectively enable the creation of robust, efficient, and maintainable Delphi applications.

The progression begins with an examination of the advanced core aspects of the Delphi language. Here, readers will gain a thorough understanding of Delphi's Pascal-based syntax, intricate block structures, and sophisticated control flow constructs. The discussion extends to the internal workings of Delphi's type system, which encompasses static and dynamic typing, as well as advanced data structures such as records, arrays, variants, and sets. Memory management is also addressed in detail, covering heap and stack allocation, manual and automatic memory control, along with performance optimization strategies. Additionally, this section delves into the design and implementation of procedures and functions, parameter passing conventions, the use of function pointers, and inline expansions. Error handling mechanisms receive particular attention, with robust approaches to exceptions, stack unwinding, and custom exception constructs that strengthen application reliability. The modularization capabilities offered by units and namespaces complete the foundational overview, providing strategies for scalable and maintainable code organization.

Building on this foundation, the text explores object-oriented programming principles as implemented in Delphi. The object model and class architecture topics include metaprogramming techniques, inheritance hierarchies, and class helpers that extend functionality. The discussion of interfaces, delegation, and abstraction highlights how Delphi facilitates powerful design abstractions, including interface delegation and interoperability with COM. The fundamentals of encapsulation, polymorphism, and controlled visibility are thoroughly explained through access specifiers, virtual methods, constructor chaining, and dynamic dispatch mechanisms. Generics introduce strong typing and reusable code components, while anonymous methods and closures expose functional programming paradigms that enhance code flexibility. Runtime type information (RTTI) and reflection capabilities are explored to showcase dynamic behaviors such as serialization and inspection, enabling adaptive application features.

In addition to language features, the book dedicates considerable focus to component-based application development within the Delphi framework. It covers component design principles and best practices for both design-time and runtime, including property editors. Deep insights into the Visual Component Library (VCL) and FireMonkey (FMX) frameworks reveal customization opportunities—from control development and message handling to cross-platform styling and 2D/3D graphics integration. The complexities of component serialization, event-driven programming, theming, styling, and accessibility considerations are addressed to equip readers with the skills necessary to produce polished, user-friendly applications.

Modern data access and multitier architecture approaches are integral to contemporary application development, and this volume offers detailed guidance on these fronts. Advanced techniques for interfacing with databases through FireDAC and dbExpress, as well as the use of object-relational mapping and entity frameworks, are presented. Architectures leveraging DataSnap, REST, SOAP, and live data feeds illustrate scalable service-oriented designs. Strategies for SQL integration, query optimization, and rigorous data validation consolidate the focus on data integrity and performance.

Networking and web application capabilities are also comprehensively covered. The treatment of socket programming, protocol design, RESTful and SOAP-based web services, and data serialization techniques addresses the demands of connected applications. Real-time communications, including WebSocket implementations and SignalR patterns, are addressed alongside critical security concepts such as cryptography, secure transports, and certificate management.

Concurrency, parallelism, and asynchronous programming represent essential competencies for scalable and responsive software. Topics include multithreading management, task-based parallelism using the TTask framework, asynchronous design patterns, thread-safe data structures, and performance tuning. Comprehensive methods for troubleshooting and deadlock detection further assist in managing complex concurrent systems.

The book also emphasizes quality assurance through advanced testing and debugging techniques. A thorough exposition of unit, integration, system, and UI testing frameworks, along with profiling and code analysis tools, supports the creation of high-confidence applications. Continuous integration and delivery pipelines are discussed to encourage modern development workflows that ensure code stability and frequent, reliable releases.

Addressing the needs of multi-platform and cloud-enabled development, the text covers mobile development for iOS and Android, integration with native libraries and APIs, cloud service consumption, deployment strategies, and application monitoring through telemetry and logging.

Finally, attention is given to sustainable software engineering practices. Secure coding techniques prevent vulnerabilities, while code organization, refactoring, documentation, and design pattern implementation foster maintainable and extensible codebases. Legal and compliance considerations provide crucial guidance for responsible software production under varying licenses and regulations.

Throughout this comprehensive exposition, *Delphi Programming Essentials* prioritizes clarity, depth, and practical applicability. It serves not only as a technical manual but as a thorough reference that equips experienced Delphi developers with the knowledge required to design, implement, and maintain sophisticated software solutions aligned with modern industry standards.

Chapter 1

Advanced Delphi Language Core

Venture beyond the basics and unlock the powerful intricacies of the Delphi language. This chapter reveals the architecture and subtle mechanics behind Delphi's Pascal roots, from type systems and memory models to robust error handling and scalable modularization. Whether you're targeting performance, code safety, or architectural clarity, these advanced language fundamentals will elevate your Delphi mastery and empower you to craft elegant, resilient solutions.

1.1. Syntax, Structure, and Program Flow

Delphi's syntax is characterized by a clear, verbose, yet flexible structure that facilitates both readability and expressive power. The fundamental unit of code organization is the *block*, enclosed within `begin` and `end` keywords. Blocks serve as containers for compound statements, enabling logical grouping and nesting of code segments. This visual and syntactic clarity distinguishes Delphi's approach to structured programming and is central to its control flow mechanisms.

A program block typically occurs within procedure or function bodies, event handlers, and anonymous methods, where multiple statements execute sequentially. The general form of a block is:

```
begin
  <statement 1>;
  <statement 2>;
  ...
  <statement n>;
end;
```

Each statement ends with a semicolon, except possibly the last in some contexts, maintaining deliberate delineation between operations.

Delphi's control flow includes a rich set of conditional and looping constructs, enhanced by nuanced language-specific idioms that maximize expressiveness and efficiency. Unlike many languages, Delphi supports both the traditional if-then-else branching and the case statement, each with distinctive syntactic and semantic properties.

The if statement syntax allows nested and chained conditions:

```
if <condition> then
  <statement 1>
else if <condition 2> then
  <statement 2>
else
  <statement 3>;
```

Each branch may be a single statement or a compound block. Notably, the then and else keywords establish execution paths explicitly, avoiding ambiguous dangling-else issues common in less formalized languages.

The case statement in Delphi permits branching on ordinal types, enumerations, or sets of discrete constants, providing efficiency benefits through jump tables or optimized dispatch logic. Its syn-

6

tax is:

```
case <expression> of
  <constant 1>: <statement list 1>;
  <constant 2>, <constant 3>: <statement list 2>;
  else
    <default statements>;
end;
```

This construct elegantly handles multi-branch conditions and can include multiple values per branch, a flexibility that streamlines code when several discrete values require identical handling.

Looping constructs exhibit significant versatility, addressing diverse iteration patterns:

- while loops evaluate the condition before executing the body, accommodating cases where zero iterations are possible.

```
while <condition> do
  <statement>;
```

- repeat-until loops execute the body at least once, testing the exit condition post-execution. This subtle difference optimizes scenarios where initial execution is mandatory before conditional checking.

```
repeat
  <statement list>;
until <condition>;
```

- for loops provide controlled iteration across ordinal ranges or enumerations, automatically incrementing or decrementing the control variable. The downto keyword introduces reverse iteration, demonstrating natural and expressively tailored looping capabilities native to Delphi.

```
for <variable> := <start> to <end> do
  <statement>;
```

```
for <variable> := <end> downto <start> do
  <statement>;
```

Beyond these classical constructs, Delphi programmers frequently leverage language-specific idioms to influence program flow more fluidly and idiomatically. For instance, the `continue` and `break` statements, though inherited from conventional procedural languages, integrate seamlessly with Delphi's structured blocks, allowing mid-loop control modification without compromising readability:

```
for i := 1 to 10 do
begin
  if SomeCondition(i) then
    continue;
  Process(i);
  if ShouldExit(i) then
    break;
end;
```

Delphi also supports *nested* and *labeled* control flows, albeit the latter is less common in modern stylistic conventions due to their potential to reduce clarity. Labels can be declared and used with `goto` statements to jump to marked positions within procedures or functions, useful in cases demanding early cleanup or complex error handling flows:

```
label ErrorHandler;

begin
  ...
  if ErrorOccurred then
    goto ErrorHandler;
  ...
  Exit;

ErrorHandler:
  HandleError;
end;
```

While `goto` should be used judiciously, its availability reflects Delphi's pragmatic balance between structured programming and low-level control.

Language-specific idioms extend to syntactic sugar for conditions, such as the with statement, which reduces verbosity when accessing properties or fields of records and objects:

```
with SomeObject do
begin
  Property1 := Value1;
  Property2 := Value2;
  MethodCall;
end;
```

This construct effectively shortens nested field references, aiding both clarity and conciseness in complex data manipulation tasks.

Handling error-prone or exceptional logic frequently involves the try-except and try-finally statements, integral to Delphi's structured exception handling paradigm. Though not classical flow control, these statements influence program execution paths significantly:

```
try
  // Code that may raise exceptions
except
  on E: ExceptionType do
    HandleException(E);
end;

try
  // Code section
finally
  CleanUpResources;
end;
```

These constructs ensure deterministic cleanup and fault tolerance in the program flow, extending Delphi's semantics far beyond simple looping or branching.

Delphi's refined syntax and structure marry classical procedural clarity with versatile, nuanced mechanisms. Blocks conjoin sequences of statements with explicit delimiters, while conditional and iterative constructs provide both simplicity and expressiveness. Specialized idioms such as with, the comprehensive case statement, and structured exception handling enhance readabil-

9

ity and control flow transparency. Understanding these elements deeply enables the crafting of robust, maintainable, and elegantly structured Delphi applications.

1.2. Type System Internals

Delphi's type system embodies a sophisticated architecture that balances static and dynamic typing mechanisms to achieve both type safety and flexibility essential for modern software design. At its core, Delphi employs static typing, where types are checked at compile-time, ensuring early detection of type mismatches. However, the language also incorporates dynamic typing features, permitting runtime type information queries and manipulations through mechanisms such as `Variant` types and Run-Time Type Information (RTTI). Understanding these internal facets is crucial to mastering the language's extensible and robust type capabilities.

Static Typing and Type Safety

Delphi's static typing enforces strict rules during compilation regarding data types, method signatures, and operator compatibility. Primitive types like `Integer`, `Char`, and `Boolean` have well-defined fixed sizes and semantics, while user-defined types such as `records`, `sets`, and `arrays` introduce compositional type structures. The compiler maintains type safety by enforcing invariant properties—for example, implicitly prohibiting assignments between incompatible types unless explicit casts or conversions are defined. This guarantees predictability and robustness in the generated code, mitigating runtime errors linked to type violations.

Advanced Usage of Records

Records in Delphi provide a potent structuring mechanism beyond simple aggregations of fields. Unlike plain structs in some languages, Delphi's records can declare methods, properties, operator overloads, and even implement interfaces, bridging the conceptual gap between structured and object-oriented paradigms. This allows records to encapsulate both data and behavior with value-type semantics, enabling efficient memory usage without the overhead of heap allocations typical of class instances.

Memory layout of records is sequential and contiguous, enabling deterministic access patterns advantageous in low-level programming and interfacing with external APIs. Records support variant parts, also known as discriminated unions, allowing conditional storage layouts based on a tag field. This mechanism facilitates memory-efficient representations of different but related data formats within the same overall record type.

Operator overloading in records empowers developers to define custom arithmetic, comparison, and assignment behaviors, integral for types representing mathematical constructs or domain-specific entities. Furthermore, records may implement interface contracts, facilitating polymorphic behavior without transitioning to reference semantics.

Arrays and Their Nuances

Delphi offers a versatile array model encompassing static, dynamic, and open arrays, each with distinct internal characteristics. Static arrays have sizes fixed at compile-time and reside on the stack or within record structures, providing predictable memory layouts and access patterns. Conversely, dynamic arrays are heap-allocated with automatic memory management; the compiler generates reference-counting code to track their usage, making them suitable for collections with mutable sizes.

The dynamic array's internal structure includes a hidden header preceding the data pointer, containing metadata such as reference count, length, and capacity. This design enables Delphi's memory manager to efficiently manage array lifetimes and optimize copy-on-write semantics, where data duplication occurs only when a shared array is modified.

Open arrays serve as a flexible parameter-passing convention, allowing procedures and functions to accept arrays of arbitrary length and type, enhancing generic programming capabilities. Type checking ensures the element types match, while runtime support provides bounds information for safe iteration.

Multi-dimensional arrays in Delphi are implemented as arrays of arrays, and their memory layout corresponds to nested sequences of elements. The indexing operations are compiled into offset calculations based on array bounds, which can be non-zero based, although zero-based arrays are common in modern practice.

Variants and Runtime Type Flexibility

Variant types in Delphi implement a form of dynamic typing by storing data that can vary in type at runtime. Internally, a Variant is a tagged union, with a type descriptor field indicating the current contained data type and a corresponding value field storing the data. The type descriptor enables the Delphi runtime to dispatch operations dynamically, such as arithmetic, comparison, or method invocations.

Variants support a broad range of types, including integer, floating-point, string, Boolean, arrays, and even references to Automation objects. The runtime employs late binding and type coercion rules to resolve operators applied to variants, providing a flexible programming model at the cost of some performance overhead compared to statically typed operations.

Advanced usage scenarios leverage variants for interfacing with COM, Automation servers, and dynamically typed languages, where compile-time type information is unavailable or impractical. Variants can represent complex data structures such as variant arrays (SAFEARRAYs), allowing Delphi applications to consume and produce inter-language and inter-process data transparently.

Sets: Compact Collections of Ordinal Types

Sets in Delphi represent collections of values from an ordinal type, typically enumerations and subranges of integers. Internally, sets are implemented as bitsets, where each possible element corresponds to a bit in a fixed-size integer or array of integers. This encoding offers a compact and efficient representation suitable for frequent membership tests, union, intersection, and difference operations, all implemented as fast bitwise operators.

The maximum size of a set is limited by the bit width of the underlying storage (commonly 256 elements), which aligns with practical requirements but differs from more flexible collection types like arrays or lists. Sets enjoy first-class syntax support, with set constructors, membership tests using the in operator, and set algebra expressions supported natively by the compiler.

Static type checking guarantees that only elements of the declared base type can be added to a set, ensuring type safety. This facilitates pattern matching, flags enumeration, and state tracking scenarios in a succinct and performant manner.

Extensibility Through Run-Time Type Information

Delphi's Run-Time Type Information (RTTI) framework supplements the static type system by embedding metadata describing types, fields, methods, and properties into the compiled executable. This metadata supports reflection, enabling runtime inspection and dynamic invocation of members, serialization, and advanced framework functionalities such as dependency injection and model-driven development.

RTTI coverage extends beyond simple types to encompass classes, records with methods, dynamic arrays, and variants, creating a cohesive type introspection system. The extensibility of RTTI is a cornerstone of Delphi's modern language features and component architecture, allowing developers to write general-purpose libraries that adapt to the type information exposed at runtime.

The interplay between static checking, dynamic typing features, and sophisticated type constructs such as enriched records, managed arrays, versatile variants, and efficient sets collectively empowers Delphi with a strong yet flexible type system. This facilitates safer code, efficient memory usage, and expressive design patterns suitable for a diverse range of application domains—from embedded systems to enterprise-scale solutions. Mastery of these internals unlocks the full potential of Delphi's type safety, extensibility, and runtime dynamism, foundational to robust and maintainable software architectures.

1.3. Memory Management Paradigms

Delphi's memory management system fundamentally integrates two predominant allocation strategies: stack allocation and heap allocation. These two paradigms serve distinct but complementary roles in managing data lifetimes and memory usage patterns within Delphi applications. Understanding the differences, efficiencies, and management techniques associated with stack and heap memory is crucial for achieving optimal performance and reliability.

The stack is a region of memory that operates in a last-in, first-out (LIFO) manner, primarily used for statically sized, short-lived data such as local variables and function call contexts. Allocation and deallocation on the stack are extremely efficient because they merely involve moving the stack pointer. In Delphi, primitive data types and record instances declared within procedure or function bodies are typically allocated on the stack. The stack's size is predetermined and significantly smaller than the heap, which restricts the amount of memory available for static allocation but guarantees deterministic lifetimes and fast access.

Conversely, the heap is a much larger pool of memory managed dynamically, designed for objects and data structures whose size or lifetime cannot be determined at compile time. Heap memory in Delphi is managed manually or semi-automatically, depending on the object type. Heap allocation requires the runtime to search for free memory blocks, allocate space, and often maintain metadata for each allocation, thereby incurring higher overhead compared to stack allocation. Objects created using the New operator or class instances instantiated via constructors are allocated on the heap. Their memory persists until explicitly freed, or until the memory manager reclaims it, introducing complexity in tracking and ensuring correct disposal.

Delphi primarily requires manual memory management for heap-allocated objects, meaning developers must invoke Free or Dispose to release memory. Failure to do so results in memory leaks, which degrade application stability and performance over time. Unlike environments with garbage collection, Delphi's manual approach provides deterministic destruction and resource release without runtime pause but places the burden of correctness and discipline on the programmer.

Nonetheless, modern Delphi versions have introduced automatic memory management for interface references via reference counting. Interfaces internally maintain a count of active references, and the memory manager automatically deallocates the object once the reference count drops to zero. This blend of automatic and manual schemes demands careful design to avoid circular references, which impede reference counting and cause memory to linger.

Optimization strategies revolve around maximizing the use of stack allocation where feasible and minimizing heap allocations, particularly in performance-critical code paths. Allocating large arrays or complex structures on the stack should be done cautiously due to fixed stack size constraints, whereas leveraging records with managed fields (e.g., strings, dynamic arrays) can provide flexibility without incurring heap overhead if properly scoped. Developers are encouraged to utilize local variables and short-lived records to benefit from stack allocation's speed and automatic cleanup.

When heap allocation is indispensable, best practices include employing centralized allocation patterns and custom memory pools to reduce fragmentation and allocation overhead. Delphi's built-in FastMM memory manager offers efficient pooling and defragmentation algorithms, but advanced scenarios benefit from explicit pooling and preallocation. Reusing objects through object pools rather than creating and destroying them repeatedly can reduce heap churn and improve cache locality.

Systematic use of `try-finally` blocks ensures that heap objects are freed reliably, avoiding leaks even in the presence of exceptions. Furthermore, Delphi's `TComponent` architecture embeds ownership semantics that assist with automatic destruction cascades, simplifying memory management within component hierarchies.

Identifying and eliminating leaks requires profiling tools specialized for Delphi, such as FastMM in debug mode, which detects leaks, double frees, and corruptions. Integration with IDE tools that monitor memory usage at runtime can guide developers to problematic code segments. Adopting coding conventions that clearly distinguish ownership and lifecycle responsibilities enhances maintainability and minimizes the risk of leaks.

The dichotomy of stack and heap memory in Delphi establishes a foundation for efficient and predictable memory usage. Manual and reference-counted techniques coexist, each suited to particular scenarios within Delphi's object model. Adhering to optimization strategies such as maximizing stack usage, minimizing heap allocations, employing ownership patterns, and leveraging robust cleanup constructs underpins high-performance, leak-free Delphi applications. These paradigms, combined with vigilant profiling and disciplined coding practices, empower developers to harness Delphi's memory architecture effectively.

1.4. Procedures, Functions, and Methodologies

Advanced procedures and functions constitute the cornerstone of modular and efficient software design. Mastery of these elements involves an intricate understanding of their implementation nuances, including function pointers, parameter passing conventions, and inline expansions. Each contributes uniquely to the goals of code organization, reuse, and high-performance abstraction.

Function pointers serve as dynamic references to executable code blocks, enabling flexible control flow and fostering extensibility. They are particularly valuable in implementing callback mechanisms, event-driven architectures, and dispatch tables. The definition of a function pointer involves capturing the signature of the target function succinctly. For instance, in a statically typed language like C, a pointer to a function returning int and accepting two int arguments is declared as:

```
int (*func_ptr)(int, int);
```

Assigning and invoking through such pointers enhances abstraction by decoupling the caller from the callee's concrete implementation. This indirection introduces runtime flexibility but entails performance trade-offs due to reduced opportunities for compiler inlining and increased call overhead, which requires judicious application in performance-critical contexts.

Parameter passing conventions dictate how arguments are transferred from caller to callee, influencing function call overhead, side effects, and data consistency. The primary mechanisms include call-by-value, call-by-reference, and call-by-const-reference (or equivalent language-specific variants). Call-by-value replicates the argument's content, safeguarding against unintended mutations yet incurring a cost proportional to data size. Conversely, call-by-reference transmits the address, enabling efficient modification of large aggregates like structures or classes but potentially introducing aliasing complexities.

In systems programming and high-performance frameworks, the choice of parameter passing technique demands a nuanced balance. For instance, passing large data structures by const-reference (in C++ or via pointers in C) curtails copying overhead while preserving immutability guarantees. Modern compilers often optimize small data types by passing them through registers, minimizing latency, but for composite types, explicit control over passing style remains consequential for performance:

```
// Pass by value: potential copy overhead
void processData(Data d);

// Pass by const reference: no copy, read-only access
void processData(const Data& d);
```

Inline expansions represent a powerful optimization where function bodies are substituted directly at call sites, eliminating call overhead and exposing opportunities for further compiler optimizations such as constant propagation and loop unrolling. Marking functions as `inline` or employing compiler-specific attributes invites the compiler to perform these expansions, although the ultimate decision resides with the optimizer.

Inlining small, frequently invoked functions such as accessors, mutators, or simple computations aligns well with performance targets. However, indiscriminate inlining of large functions inflates binary size and may degrade instruction cache efficiency. Additionally, inline expansions facilitate more aggressive interprocedural optimizations by revealing function internals to the compiler earlier.

The orchestration of these techniques underpins effective code organization and reuse. By defining clean, reusable interfaces through well-parameterized functions and advocating abstraction capabilities via function pointers or higher-order functions, software systems achieve modularity. This modularity succinctly isolates changes, promotes testability, and enables polymorphism, both at compile-time and runtime.

For example, an abstract machine interface employing function pointers for operations like `initialize`, `execute`, and `cleanup` can dynamically bind to different implementations without recompilation. This pattern is quintessential in plugin architectures and embedded systems where code size and flexibility constraints co-exist.

High-performance abstractions further arise from combining inline expansions with advanced parameter passing. Template metaprogramming in C++ exploits compile-time composition of operations, often resolved entirely through inlining, yielding zero-overhead abstractions. Such paradigms blur the line between code reuse and raw performance by allowing generic constructs that compile away to specialized, optimized code fragments.

In contrast, languages supporting first-class functions and closures abstract procedures as data, further extending reuse capabilities. While the associated runtime cost of closure allocations can be minimized by compiler escape analysis and stack allocation strategies, the invocation mechanics typically leverage the concept of function pointers or their runtime analogs.

To summarize the interdependencies, consider the typical performance-aware function design guidelines:

- Minimize copies by using references or pointers for large data types unless mutation safety requires value copying.

- Use inline expansions for trivial or performance-critical functions to reduce call overhead and enable optimization.

- Employ function pointers judiciously for flexibility but be aware of their cost in predicted call path optimizations.

- Leverage language features such as template inlining or lambdas to combine abstraction and performance.

- Structure code modularly to maximize reuse while allowing the compiler to optimize hot paths effectively.

The overarching methodology involves iteratively profiling, refactoring, and tuning function interfaces to align with the application's performance envelope while preserving clarity and maintainability. Understanding the interplay between calling conventions, function pointer usage, and inline expansion is imperative for creating sophisticated, efficient software architectures that scale in complexity without compromising execution speed.

1.5. Exception and Error Handling

Robustness and resilience in Delphi applications hinge on the ability to systematically handle exceptional conditions and errors that may arise during runtime. A comprehensive approach to exception and error handling demands mastery of several advanced concepts: thorough exception capture, the creation of custom exception classes tailored to application semantics, controlled stack unwinding, and rigorous error propagation strategies. These are critical in mission-critical systems where graceful degradation and error traceability directly affect reliability and maintainability.

Delphi's native exception mechanism is built around the try-except and try-finally constructs, which can be leveraged not only for error detection but for structured and recoverable error management. While try-except allows handling and recovery from exceptions, try-finally enforces the execution of cleanup code regardless of the occurrence of exceptions, ensuring resource integrity even in the presence of faults.

```
try
  // code that might raise exception
except
```

20

```
  on E: EDivByZero do
    ShowMessage('Division by zero error.');
  on E: Exception do
    ShowMessage('General exception: ' + E.Message);
end;
```

Capturing exceptions at the appropriate granularity is paramount. Overly broad handling can obscure the root cause and complicate debugging, whereas overly narrow handling can let critical issues pass unchecked. Therefore, it is recommended to handle specific, expected exceptions close to their source while allowing unexpected exceptions to propagate to higher-level handlers or global exception managers.

Custom exception classes extend the base Exception class, enabling the encapsulation of domain-specific error data and behaviors. Defining such exceptions brings clarity and precision to error classification, facilitating targeted handling and richer diagnostics.

```
type
  EDatabaseError = class(Exception)
  private
    FErrorCode: Integer;
  public
    constructor Create(const Msg: string; Code: Integer);
    property ErrorCode: Integer read FErrorCode;
  end;

constructor EDatabaseError.Create(const Msg: string; Code:
    Integer);
begin
  inherited Create(Msg);
  FErrorCode := Code;
end;
```

Using custom exceptions improves error reporting and aligns error handling workflows with application-specific semantics. For example, a data access layer can raise EDatabaseError with specific error codes that higher layers interpret for corrective actions or logging.

Stack unwinding in Delphi occurs automatically when exceptions propagate. Each invocation context is popped off the call stack

21

as the exception travels upward until it finds an appropriate handler. Proper use of `try-finally` blocks ensures that necessary cleanups—such as freeing dynamically allocated objects, closing files, or rolling back transactions—are performed during unwinding, preserving system integrity and preventing resource leaks.

A nuanced aspect of robustness is error propagation strategy design. In mission-critical systems, controlled propagation is required to avoid silent failures or uncontrolled aborts. A common pattern is to catch exceptions at module boundaries, wrap them in higher-level exceptions with enriched context, and re-raise them to maintain a comprehensive error chain.

```
try
  DataModule.LoadConfiguration;
except
  on E: Exception do
    raise EConfigurationLoadError.Create('Error loading
    configuration: ' + E.Message);
end;
```

This approach preserves the original cause while providing additional insights to the caller, facilitating fault diagnosis without sacrificing abstraction barriers.

Global exception handling complements localized strategies by capturing uncaught exceptions, often to log detailed diagnostics and perform fail-safe measures. Depending on the Delphi application type (VCL, FMX, Console), the global exception handler is set using `Application.OnException` or by installing an OS-level handler. Missions with high availability requirements may implement watchdog mechanisms within these handlers to trigger restarts or alert operators.

To further enhance fault tolerance, transactional or compensating patterns should be incorporated where applicable. For instance, database operations wrapped in transactions should use exceptions to trigger rollbacks. The following code snippet demonstrates this principle:

```
try
  Database.StartTransaction;
  try
    BusinessLogic.PerformUpdates;
    Database.Commit;
  except
    on E: Exception do
    begin
      Database.Rollback;
      raise; // propagate exception after rollback
    end;
  end;
except
  on E: Exception do
    LogError('Transaction failed: ' + E.Message);
end;
```

This layered usage ensures rollback consistency even when nested exceptions arise, while propagating errors for higher-level management.

In addition to these coding patterns, the design of extensive error logging and reporting is indispensable. Exception objects carry textual descriptions and can be extended with contextual metadata such as call stack snapshots, error codes, and timestamps. Instrumenting applications to capture this information in persistent logs or telemetry streams facilitates postmortem analysis and proactive problem resolution.

Delivering resilient Delphi applications for mission-critical environments requires embracing an advanced error handling discipline:

- Define and utilize custom exceptions to capture domain-specific conditions precisely.

- Design hierarchical error propagation that enriches context without losing root causes.

- Employ stack unwinding mechanisms and try-finally constructs to guarantee resource cleanup.

- Implement global handlers combined with comprehensive

logging to manage unexpected failures gracefully.

These strategies collectively support the robustness and maintainability necessary in demanding production systems.

1.6. Units, Namespaces, and Modularization

Delphi's modular programming model centers on the concept of *units*—self-contained source files that encapsulate interface and implementation details. Units are the fundamental building blocks that enable developers to organize code logically and promote reuse, separation of concerns, and maintainability. A well-structured application divides its functionality across multiple units, each representing a cohesive module or feature, thereby simplifying development and evolution over time.

A Delphi unit consists primarily of two sections: the `interface` section, which declares public types, variables, constants, procedures, functions, and classes; and the `implementation` section, which contains the actual algorithmic code and data that support the interface declarations. This division permits information hiding, as only the interface elements are visible to other units, preventing unintended coupling and fostering encapsulation.

The basic skeleton of a Delphi unit is depicted below:

```
unit UnitName;

interface

uses
  DependencyUnits;

type
  TExample = class
    procedure DoSomething;
  end;

implementation

procedure TExample.DoSomething;
```

```
begin
  // method implementation
end;

end.
```

In this structure, the uses clause in the interface section declares dependencies on other units whose types or functions are referenced in the interface. A separate uses clause within the implementation section specifies additional dependencies used internally, allowing for finer control over visibility and compilation dependencies.

Managing dependencies carefully is critical in scalable Delphi projects. Circular references between units must be avoided as the Delphi compiler requires a clear, acyclic dependency graph. This often necessitates forward declarations or isolating shared interfaces into dedicated units to reduce tight coupling. Component designers and library authors frequently place abstract base classes or interface declarations in separate units that both clients and implementers can reference without creating circularity.

Namespaces in Delphi were introduced to provide an additional mechanism for grouping and disambiguating identifiers. Unlike some languages where namespaces are runtime constructs, Delphi namespaces are primarily a compile-time organizational facility linked to unit naming conventions. They allow large frameworks or applications to segment units hierarchically, using dot-separated identifiers to form qualified unit names such as:

```
Vcl.Controls, System.SysUtils, MyApp.Core.Logging
```

Using namespaces helps prevent name collisions, especially when integrating third-party libraries. Developers can resolve ambiguous identifiers by qualifying them with their namespace or by using appropriate uses clauses, which can specify unit names with or without their full namespace qualifiers depending on the context.

To create a unit with a namespace, the unit name in the unit statement must include the full qualifier:

```
unit MyApp.Core.Logging;
```

This convention enforces a directory structure matching the namespace path, supporting automated project builds and clearer source code organization. The use of namespaces is particularly advantageous when modularizing large applications or frameworks distributed as packages, where shared units might otherwise conflict.

Delphi's package system extends the modularization capabilities by enabling compiled units to be grouped into packages (.BPL files). Packages facilitate component distribution, dynamic loading, and version management of modular libraries. Units within a package can share internal units accessible only to other units in the same package, enforcing encapsulation boundaries and reducing external dependencies.

Effective modularization also leverages *interface-based programming*, a paradigm where units expose functionality solely through well-defined interfaces. Interfaces are reference-counted and decoupled from concrete implementations, allowing runtime substitution and version-independent client code. Declaring interfaces within dedicated units and referencing them via namespace-qualified unit names supports clean dependency management and incremental system evolution.

The organization of units, namespaces, and dependencies directly impacts compile-time performance. Careful architecture aims to minimize units with extensive interface uses clauses, thus reducing recompilation cascades. Smaller, focused units with clearly defined interfaces and minimal reliance on heavy dependencies yield faster build times and facilitate parallel development.

Mastering Delphi's units and namespaces entails:

- Structuring code into coherent units with clear interface and implementation separation.

- Using uses clauses judiciously to manage dependencies and prevent circular references.

- Applying namespaces to group units logically and avoid naming conflicts.

- Encapsulating shared abstractions in dedicated units to promote reusability and reduce coupling.

- Leveraging packages for modular deployment and encapsulation beyond unit boundaries.

- Emphasizing interface-based designs to enable flexible and maintainable software architectures.

Through these modular programming constructs, Delphi provides the foundational tools necessary to build large-scale, maintainable applications that evolve gracefully over time while preserving code clarity and compilation efficiency.

Chapter 2

Object-Oriented Programming with Delphi

Delphi's object-oriented strengths transcend tradition, enabling developers to architect elegant, modular, and high-performance software. This chapter unlocks advanced techniques—from deep class hierarchies and flexible interfaces to powerful runtime introspection—teaching you to mold the language's OOP features into solutions that are both robust and adaptable. Unleash the full potential of Delphi's object model and elevate your applications to new heights of sophistication.

2.1. Class Architecture and Object Model

Delphi's class system is the foundation upon which its object-oriented capabilities are built, providing a rich and flexible framework to model complex application domains. At the core of this system lies the concept of the *class*, which serves not only as a blueprint for object instantiation but also as a runtime entity with metadata, facilitating advanced patterns such as reflection, dynamic creation, and extensibility mechanisms.

A Delphi class internally comprises two main components: the VMT (Virtual Method Table), which supports dynamic dispatch of methods, and a metaclass structure, enabling operations on class types as first-class objects. This duality is critical for Delphi's rich type information and dynamic behavior. Metaclasses, created as descendants of TClass, embody the runtime representation of classes themselves, allowing patterns like factory creation and class registration to be implemented seamlessly.

Inheritance in Delphi is strictly single and supports both implementation inheritance and polymorphism. Each class implicitly inherits from a base TObject, which provides fundamental methods such as Create, Destroy, ClassName, and ClassType. These inherited behaviors establish a consistent object lifecycle and introspection model across all user-defined types. The inheritance mechanism is designed to facilitate extensibility, enabling developers to override virtual methods to extend or modify behavior without altering the original class code.

Delphi further enriches inheritance with *class helpers*, a unique feature that allows the extension of existing classes (including RTL and VCL classes) without modifying their source. Class helpers operate as lightweight intermediaries, offering new methods scoped to the helper's visibility. They adhere to strict conflict resolution rules-only a single helper is active for any given class within a compilation unit, ensuring predictability. This capability is instrumental for inserting cross-cutting behaviors or adapting third-party classes in a non-intrusive manner.

A nuanced understanding of Delphi's object lifecycle management reveals sophisticated mechanisms beyond simple construction and destruction sequences. Delphi encourages explicit implementation of constructors and destructors with virtual dispatch to ensure that initialization and cleanup properly cascade through the inheritance chain. Moreover, the introduction of class operators enables more flexible instantiation patterns, such as factory methods or cloning semantics. The management of object references is traditionally manual, but Delphi's supporting frameworks, like Automatic Reference Counting (ARC) on mobile platforms, illustrate extended lifecycle management strategies that coexist with the classic model.

Designing extensible and maintainable class hierarchies in Delphi relies on thoughtful application of these architectural elements. A robust class design leverages inheritance sparingly and strategically, favoring composition and interfaces when appropriate to reduce coupling and support polymorphic behavior without deep inheritance chains. Choosing when and how to utilize virtual methods, abstract classes, and overridden constructors directly impacts the flexibility and clarity of the resulting hierarchy.

Consider the example of designing a component framework. The base component class, inheriting from TObject, defines a minimal interface for lifecycle events and common functionality such as notification and persistence. Derived classes then extend this interface with domain-specific behaviors, using overridden virtual methods to customize initialization, rendering, or event handling stages. Employing class helpers provides an avenue to augment components with additional capabilities, such as logging or debugging utilities, without affecting the core inheritance structure.

To illustrate the metaclass and class helper concepts succinctly, the following code snippet defines a base TAnimal class with virtual behavior, a derived TDog class overriding that behavior, and a helper for TAnimal introducing a new method:

```
type
  TAnimal = class
  public
    procedure Speak; virtual;
    class procedure Factory; virtual;
```

31

```
  end;

  TDog = class(TAnimal)
  public
    procedure Speak; override;
  end;

  TAnimalHelper = class helper for TAnimal
    procedure Eat;
  end;

procedure TAnimal.Speak;
begin
  WriteLn('An animal makes a sound.');
end;

procedure TDog.Speak;
begin
  WriteLn('The dog barks.');
end;

class procedure TAnimal.Factory;
var
  AnimalClass: TClass;
  Animal: TAnimal;
begin
  // Create instance dynamically using metaclass
  AnimalClass := TDog;
  Animal := TAnimal(AnimalClass.Create);
  try
    Animal.Speak;
    // Uses the helper method
    (Animal as TAnimal).Eat;
  finally
    Animal.Free;
  end;
end;

procedure TAnimalHelper.Eat;
begin
  WriteLn('Eating food.');
end;
```

When the Factory method executes, the output is:

```
The dog barks.
Eating food.
```

This code encapsulates the interplay between classes, metaclasses, virtual methods, and class helpers: the metaclass TClass enables runtime type creation; virtual methods allow polymorphic behavior; the helper extends the API without altering inheritance, all while maintaining strict lifecycle management through `Create` and `Free`.

Delphi's class and object model emphasizes clarity, runtime flexibility, and maintainability by integrating classical object-oriented principles with innovative language constructs. Mastery of metaclasses, inheritance strategies, class helpers, and lifecycle semantics empowers developers to architect complex, extensible systems that stand the test of evolving requirements and platform changes.

2.2. Interfaces, Delegation, and Abstraction

Delphi's interface constructs provide a robust foundation for implementing true abstraction and decoupling in software design. Unlike class inheritance, interfaces define contracts without implementation details, enabling modular and maintainable architectures where components interact through well-defined boundaries.

An interface in Delphi is declared using the `interface` keyword, followed by method signatures without implementation. For example, a simple interface for a data provider might be declared as:

```
type
  IDataProvider = interface
    ['{A7F7B9E3-0F6C-4A6F-B2A3-2C8DFFED1F01}']
    function GetData: string;
  end;
```

The GUID within square brackets uniquely identifies the interface, facilitating COM interoperability and interface querying mechanisms through `QueryInterface`. Interfaces use reference-counted memory management; the underlying compiler-generated `IUnknown` methods ensure automatic lifetime control without explicit `AddRef` or `Release` calls by the developer.

Implementing an interface requires defining a class that specifies the interface methods:

```
type
  TFileDataProvider = class(TInterfacedObject, IDataProvider)
  public
    function GetData: string;
  end;

function TFileDataProvider.GetData: string;
begin
  Result := 'Data from file';
end;
```

Here, `TInterfacedObject` provides an out-of-the-box implementation of `IUnknown`, enabling straightforward interface implementation without boilerplate code. By programming against the `IDataProvider` interface instead of the concrete `TFileDataProvider` class, client code remains decoupled from specific implementations, enhancing flexibility and testability.

Interface delegation further enriches modular design by allowing a class to forward interface method calls to another object that implements the interface. This pattern supports composition over inheritance, facilitating runtime behavior composition and separation of concerns. Delphi simplifies delegation through the `implements` keyword:

```
type
  TDataManager = class(TInterfacedObject, IDataProvider)
  private
    FProvider: IDataProvider;
  public
    constructor Create(AProvider: IDataProvider);
    // Delegates IDataProvider methods to FProvider
    property Provider: IDataProvider read FProvider implements
     IDataProvider;
  end;

constructor TDataManager.Create(AProvider: IDataProvider);
begin
  inherited Create;
  FProvider := AProvider;
end;
```

In this example, `TDataManager` exposes `IDataProvider` by

delegating all interface calls to `FProvider`. Clients consuming `TDataManager` remain unaware of the delegation, allowing flexible substitution and extensibility without subclassing. Delegation is particularly valuable in scenarios requiring dynamic behavior composition or cross-cutting concerns, such as logging or authorization.

Beyond pure Delphi usage, interfaces serve as a gateway to integrate with legacy and cross-language components through the Component Object Model (COM). Delphi's native support for COM interfaces permits seamless interoperability with COM servers, ActiveX controls, and automation objects, facilitating reuse and integration in heterogeneous environments. COM interfaces are identified by GUIDs and inherit from `IUnknown`, aligning naturally with Delphi's interface model.

To consume a COM interface in Delphi, the interface import mechanism generates corresponding Delphi interface wrappers with proper type information. Consider interaction with a COM object exposing an interface `IMathOperations`:

```
type
  IMathOperations = interface(IUnknown)
    ['{D3C4ADF6-8B19-11D2-8BCF-00A0C9C4E3D2}']
    function Add(A, B: Integer): Integer; stdcall;
  end;

var
  MathObj: IMathOperations;
begin
  // Assume CoCreateInstance has been called to initialize
     MathObj
  Writeln('Sum: ', MathObj.Add(5, 7));
end;
```

COM interoperability requires adherence to calling conventions (commonly `stdcall`), proper interface inheritance, and reference counting semantics. Delphi automates much of this boilerplate, enabling native-style interface usage with COM components.

Furthermore, Delphi interfaces support aggregated and marshaled

35

objects, empowering advanced scenarios such as distributed object communication and cross-process method invocation. This capability extends interface-based design principles beyond local contexts to broader, scalable architectures.

Delphi's interface support embodies the principles of abstraction and decoupling by defining strict contracts that isolate implementation details. Delegation enhances architectural flexibility by enabling composition of behaviors. The intrinsic alignment with COM interfaces positions Delphi as a powerful technology for integrating modern applications with legacy systems and heterogeneous software environments, unifying object-oriented design with practical interoperability.

2.3. Encapsulation, Polymorphism, and Visibility

Encapsulation serves as a fundamental principle in object-oriented design, addressing the protection of an object's internal state by controlling access to its data and behavior. This protective mechanism is achieved primarily through the use of access specifiers, commonly `private`, `protected`, and `public`, which regulate the visibility of class members. Encapsulation ensures that objects expose well-defined interfaces while concealing their internal complexities, thereby maintaining invariants and reducing dependencies between components.

The `private` specifier confers the strictest level of protection, allowing class members to be accessible only within the defining class. This restriction prevents external components or subclasses from directly modifying critical state variables, anchoring the control flow firmly within the class's own methods. The `protected` specifier extends limited visibility to derived classes while still hiding members from unrelated external access. This selective exposure fosters controlled extension of class behavior via inheritance, critical for designing robust class hierarchies. Finally, `public` members constitute the external interface, defining how clients interact with the object.

Virtual methods embody a pivotal mechanism by which encapsulation combines with polymorphism to enable dynamic behavioral extension. Declaring a method as `virtual` signals that derived classes can override the original implementation, enabling runtime dispatch to the most specific version appropriate to the actual object's type. This dynamic dispatch capability crucially supports substitutability and modularity, allowing systems to evolve through subclassing without altering existing client code. Consider the following illustrative example in C++ that highlights the interplay between encapsulation, virtual methods, and dynamic dispatch:

```
class Shape {
private:
    int id; // unique identifier, encapsulated
protected:
    virtual void draw() const {
        // default implementation
    }
public:
    Shape(int i) : id(i) {}
    virtual ~Shape() {}
    void render() const {
        draw(); // dynamic dispatch occurs here
    }
};

class Circle : public Shape {
private:
    double radius; // encapsulated radius
protected:
    void draw() const override {
        // Circle-specific drawing code
    }
public:
    Circle(int i, double r) : Shape(i), radius(r) {}
};
```

In this design, the `Shape` base class hides its internal `id` member yet provides the public method `render` responsible for invoking the virtual `draw()` method. Subclasses such as `Circle` extend

37

functionality by overriding draw(), while maintaining encapsulation of their additional state (radius). The call to render() on a Shape pointer or reference will invoke the correct draw() variant at runtime-a clear demonstration of dynamic dispatch enabling flexible and safe extension.

Constructor chaining is another critical technique closely linked to encapsulation, enabling the orderly initialization of object state across inheritance hierarchies. When an object of a derived class is instantiated, constructors are invoked in a chain starting from the most base class up to the most derived. This sequencing ensures that each class is responsible for initializing its own members before derived classes build upon this foundation. Constructor chaining preserves encapsulation by confining initialization logic within each class's constructor and mitigating the risk of incomplete or inconsistent states.

This mechanism also seamlessly integrates with polymorphic designs. Base class constructors initialize common state, while derived constructors handle specialization without compromising encapsulation. Consider the constructor chaining apparent in the preceding example, where Circle invokes Shape's constructor explicitly in its initialization list:

```
Circle(int i, double r) : Shape(i), radius(r) {}
```

This exemplifies disciplined state construction, where every class asserts clear responsibility for its encapsulated parts.

Designing for polymorphism involves careful consideration of both visibility and method binding. While virtual functions facilitate dynamic dispatch and flexible behavior extension, non-virtual functions are bound statically, limiting adaptability at runtime. Marking methods virtual must be deliberate, accounting for performance implications alongside design needs. Polymorphism encourages the use of interfaces or abstract base classes to define contracts without revealing implementation

38

details, thereby preserving encapsulation at both compile time and runtime.

An advanced application of these concepts arises in object composition and the use of interface-driven designs. By exposing only abstract interfaces (`public` and `pure virtual` methods) and hiding implementation beneath layers of encapsulation, developers produce modular components that can be replaced or extended independently. Virtual destructors are essential in such hierarchies, ensuring that destructors of derived classes are invoked correctly when deleting objects through base class pointers, preventing resource leaks and maintaining consistent object teardown.

Encapsulation enforced by access specifiers safeguards object state, while virtual methods and constructor chaining enable controlled extension and reliable initialization, respectively. Dynamic dispatch, a consequence of polymorphism, empowers objects to adapt behavior transparently, facilitating systems designed for evolution and maintainability. Mastery of these mechanisms underpins the creation of resilient and extensible software architectures.

2.4. Generics and Parameterized Types

Generics in Delphi provide a powerful mechanism for defining algorithms and data structures that operate on a variety of types while preserving strong typing and avoiding code duplication. By parameterizing types, generics enable the creation of flexible, reusable components that are both type-safe and performant. This section explores the foundational concepts of generic type creation, specialization, constraints that ensure correctness, and practical applications that promote scalability and safety in Delphi programming.

A generic type or method declaration introduces one or more type parameters, representing placeholders for types that will be specified at usage. The syntax employs angle brackets < > to enclose type parameters following the identifier. Consider the definition of a generic list that can store elements of any specified type:

```
type
  TList<T> = class
  private
    FItems: array of T;
    FCount: Integer;
  public
    procedure Add(const Item: T);
    function Get(Index: Integer): T;
    property Count: Integer read FCount;
  end;
```

Here, T acts as a type parameter, enabling TList to be instantiated for any type, such as TList<Integer> or TList<String>. This avoids the need for multiple, type-specific list implementations and maintains compile-time type safety without resorting to untyped pointers or variants.

Generic specialization occurs when a concrete type is supplied for a generic parameter, resulting in a unique class or method tailored to that type. This specialization can facilitate optimizations and type-checking at compile time. For example:

```
var
  IntList: TList<Integer>;
  StrList: TList<String>;
begin
  IntList := TList<Integer>.Create;
  IntList.Add(42);
  StrList := TList<String>.Create;
  StrList.Add('Generics');
end;
```

Delphi supports constraints on generic parameters to restrict permitted types and enforce interface or class structure expectations. Constraints improve program robustness by preventing invalid types from being used with generics and enabling safe use of specific methods or properties intrinsic to those types. Common constraints include:

- `class` - restricts the parameter to a class type (reference type).

- `record` - restricts to value types.

- `constructor` - requires a public parameterless constructor.

- `interface` - restricts to types implementing a specific interface.

An illustration of using constraints to ensure a generic type supports instantiation and a specific interface might be:

```
type
  IMyInterface = interface
    procedure DoWork;
  end;

  TWorker<T: class, constructor, IMyInterface> = class
  private
    FInstance: T;
  public
    constructor Create;
    procedure Execute;
  end;

constructor TWorker<T>.Create;
begin
  FInstance := T.Create;
end;

procedure TWorker<T>.Execute;
begin
  FInstance.DoWork;
end;
```

This pattern guarantees that any T used with TWorker implements IMyInterface, can be instantiated via a parameterless constructor, and is a class type, allowing safe invocation of interface methods and construction without reflection or unsafe casting.

Generics extend beyond classes into methods and records, further broadening reusability. Generic methods may be declared in both generic and non-generic classes, permitting algorithms to operate generically without necessitating a type-specific container. For instance, a generic method to swap two variables:

```
procedure Swap<T>(var A, B: T);
var
  Temp: T;
begin
  Temp := A;
  A := B;
  B := Temp;
end;
```

This method can be used with any assignable type, offering uniform, type-safe functionality absent manual overload definitions.

Category-specific generic data structures encompass key-value maps (TDictionary<TKey, TValue>), sets (TSet<T>), and sorted collections (TSortedList<TKey, TValue>), each leveraging generics for enhanced type clarity and safety. Utilizing these standard generic containers as building blocks promotes scalable, maintainable codebases.

Despite generics' abstraction and reusability, certain pitfalls must be managed. Runtime type information (RTTI) availability may be constrained for generic types, affecting reflection. Additionally, specialization for managed types (e.g., strings, dynamic arrays) requires attention to memory ownership semantics during element assignment and destruction to prevent leaks or access violations. Adherence to clear ownership rules and implementation of Finalize methods for generic records are recommended best practices.

In practical application, generics allow creation of strongly typed algorithms, such as sorting, searching, and filtering, without sacrificing performance or safety. For instance, a generic comparer class:

```
type
  TComparer<T> = class
  public
    class function Compare(const Left, Right: T): Integer;
      virtual; abstract;
```

```
  end;

  TIntegerComparer = class(TComparer<Integer>)
  public
    class function Compare(const Left, Right: Integer): Integer;
      override;
  end;

class function TIntegerComparer.Compare(const Left, Right:
    Integer): Integer;
begin
  if Left < Right then
    Result := -1
  else if Left > Right then
    Result := 1
  else
    Result := 0;
end;
```

Combining generic comparers with generic containers creates highly adaptable frameworks supporting reusable, extensible components. Developers can provide their own comparison logic, ensuring algorithms adapt smoothly to domain-specific requirements.

Mastery of generics and parameterized types empowers Delphi programmers to architect sophisticated, type-safe algorithms and data structures with minimal duplication and maximal scalability. Generic constraints enforce correctness, while specialization ensures optimized code generation. The interplay of generic classes, methods, and system containers forms a foundation for expressive, robust software design in contemporary Delphi development.

2.5. Anonymous Methods and Closures

Delphi's support for anonymous methods introduces a powerful functional programming paradigm seamlessly integrated within its familiar object-oriented environment. Anonymous methods are essentially code blocks defined inline, without a specific method name, that can be assigned to variables, passed as parameters, and invoked dynamically. This feature enhances expressiveness by enabling concise callback mechanisms and fostering clean event-driven and parallel programming patterns.

Definition and Syntax

An anonymous method in Delphi is declared using the `reference to` syntax, associating a procedural or function type with an unnamed code block. The general form is:

```
type
  TProc = reference to procedure;
  TFunc = reference to function(x: Integer): Integer;
```

A variable of these types can hold an anonymous method instance, as demonstrated:

```
var
  MyProc: TProc;
begin
  MyProc := procedure
    begin
      WriteLn('Anonymous method called');
    end;

  MyProc(); // Invocation
end;
```

Such constructs allow writing inline routines without verbose declarations, reducing boilerplate and enhancing clarity-especially in event handlers and short-term callbacks.

Closures: Capturing Scope and Variable Lifetimes

One of the most significant capabilities of anonymous methods in Delphi is their support for closures. A closure is an anonymous method that "captures" variables from its declaring lexical scope, preserving their state beyond typical function boundaries. This extends variable lifetimes and facilitates deferred computations or context-sensitive callbacks.

Consider the example below:

```
function MakeAdder(X: Integer): TFunc;
begin
```

```
    Result := function(Y: Integer): Integer
      begin
        Result := X + Y; // 'X' captured from surrounding scope
      end;
end;

var
  Adder: TFunc;
begin
  Adder := MakeAdder(10);
  WriteLn(Adder(5));  // Outputs 15
end;
```

Here, the anonymous function captures the parameter X from
MakeAdder's scope. Importantly, this captured variable persists as
long as the closure exists. This behavior contrasts with classical
method pointers that only reference methods of objects, without
preserving external local states.

Delphi handles captured variables with an underlying heap-
allocated context record. Each captured variable is stored in this
context, ensuring referential integrity even if the original stack
frame is gone. Consequently, modifying a captured variable
within an anonymous method affects all closures sharing that
context.

Memory Management and Reference Counting

Anonymous methods in Delphi are fundamentally implemented as
reference-counted interface types. This implies that they support
automatic memory management without explicit manual deallocation. Assigning an anonymous method to a reference to variable
increments its reference count; when the last reference disappears,
the closure's context and code block are freed automatically.

This mechanism enables safe usage of closures in asynchronous or
parallel scenarios, as the closure's lifetime neatly correlates with
active references.

However, capturing local object references inside closures
demands caution to avoid cyclic references, which can cause

45

memory leaks. To mitigate this, weak references or interfaces should be employed carefully.

Idiomatic Usage in Event-Driven Programming

Anonymous methods greatly simplify event handler implementations. Instead of declaring separate named procedures, event handlers can be defined inline at the point of assignment. This promotes locality of logic and reduces fragmentation.

For example:

```
Button1.OnClick := procedure(Sender: TObject)
begin
  ShowMessage('Button clicked');
end;
```

Here, the event handler code is directly associated with the event, improving code readability. Furthermore, closures can capture form fields or local variables, enabling customized, contextual responses without auxiliary scaffolding.

Parallelism and Task-Based Programming

Delphi's parallel programming library (`System.Threading`) leverages anonymous methods for specifying the workload in a concise manner. Tasks and parallel loops accept anonymous procedures, offering an elegant way to express concurrency.

For instance:

```
TTask.Run(procedure
begin
  // Long-running background operation
  ProcessData();
end);
```

In this scenario, the anonymous procedure passed to `TTask.Run` captures any necessary local state, allowing encapsulation of task-specific data without class fields or global variables.

Additionally, `TParallel.For` builds upon this paradigm:

```
TParallel.For(0, 99,
```

```
procedure(Index: Integer)
begin
  ProcessElement(Index);
end);
```

This idiom enhances parallelism expressiveness while maintaining clean and type-safe constructs.

Capture Rules and Limitations

While anonymous methods capture variables by reference, Delphi does not support capturing the Self pointer implicitly inside anonymous methods declared within a class method. To access instance fields or methods, the closure must be declared inside the context where Self is valid, or Self must be explicitly captured via a local variable.

Moreover, careful management of captured variables is required when closures are used in long-living contexts or asynchronous callbacks. Since the captured context creates references to variables or objects, premature object destruction can lead to invalid access or runtime errors.

By integrating anonymous methods and closures, Delphi offers developers potent tools for functional-style programming within its imperative and object-oriented framework. These constructs improve code modularity, encourage immutability patterns, and streamline asynchronous and event-driven designs. Mastery of closure capture semantics, reference counting, and idiomatic usage unlocks concise, expressive, and efficient applications across diverse programming domains.

2.6. RTTI and Reflection

Delphi's Runtime Type Information (RTTI) provides a powerful mechanism for introspection and dynamic interaction with types during program execution. Unlike static type systems, RTTI per-

47

mits exploration and manipulation of type metadata at runtime, enabling advanced programming paradigms such as dynamic behavior adaptation, custom serialization, and deep inspection that surpass static compile-time capabilities.

At the core of Delphi's RTTI system lies the TRttiContext class, which acts as the gateway to the rich repository of RTTI metadata. This context provides access to various representations of type information, including classes, records, enumerations, methods, properties, and fields. For example, obtaining the TRttiType instance for a given value, class, or type name allows subsequent discovery of its members and attributes:

```
var
  ctx: TRttiContext;
  rttiType: TRttiType;
begin
  ctx := TRttiContext.Create;
  try
    rttiType := ctx.GetType(TMyClass);
    // Further reflection operations here
  finally
    ctx.Free;
  end;
end;
```

The power of RTTI manifests when manipulating class properties dynamically at runtime. Each property can be enumerated via TRttiProperty objects. Their value can be read or assigned using GetValue and SetValue methods respectively. These can operate on actual instances regardless of the concrete type, facilitating generic algorithms:

```
var
  prop: TRttiProperty;
  instance: TObject;
  val: TValue;
begin
  instance := TMyClass.Create;
  for prop in rttiType.GetProperties do
  begin
    if prop.IsReadable then
    begin
      val := prop.GetValue(instance);
      // Example: log or transform val
```

48

```
    end;

  if prop.IsWritable then
      prop.SetValue(instance, desiredValue);
  end;
end;
```

This dynamic property manipulation forms the foundation for custom serialization frameworks. Instead of relying on fixed serialization schemas, developers can traverse an object's properties at runtime to convert it into textual or binary formats. This approach accommodates versioning changes and complex object graphs without recompilation. One widely adopted pattern involves recursively inspecting the object graph, serializing primitive properties directly, while navigating deeper into nested referenced objects:

```
procedure SerializeObject(Obj: TObject; Stream: TStream; Ctx:
    TRttiContext);
var
  Typ: TRttiType;
  Prop: TRttiProperty;
  Val: TValue;
begin
  Typ := Ctx.GetType(Obj.ClassType);
  for Prop in Typ.GetProperties do
  begin
    if Prop.IsReadable then
    begin
      Val := Prop.GetValue(Obj);
      if Val.IsObject then
        SerializeObject(Val.AsObject, Stream, Ctx)
      else
        WriteValueToStream(Val, Stream); // custom method for
    primitives
    end;
  end;
end;
```

Beyond serialization, RTTI enables sophisticated runtime inspection and modification. Reflection can query method signatures, parameter lists, and even invoke methods dynamically. This capability is central to building extensible frameworks such as dependency injection containers, event dispatchers, and scriptable components. For example, invoking a method by name at runtime

49

is straightforward:

```
var
  method: TRttiMethod;
  result: TValue;
  instance: TObject;
begin
  method := rttiType.GetMethod('ExecuteTask');
  if Assigned(method) and method.IsPublic then
  begin
    result := method.Invoke(instance, []); // no parameters
    // process result
  end;
end;
```

Moreover, Delphi RTTI supports attribute discovery, an abstraction that allows attaching declarative metadata to classes, methods, or properties. These attributes, retrieved via RTTI, enrich metadata beyond structural information, enabling behavior injection or declarative configuration:

```
type
  MySerializable = class(TCustomAttribute);

  TSample = class
  private
    [MySerializable]
    FData: string;
  end;
```

At runtime, such attributes can be detected selectively, allowing frameworks to adapt behavior accordingly without intrusive code changes. This also facilitates domain-specific language implementations, validation frameworks, and aspect-oriented programming techniques.

From a performance standpoint, RTTI operations introduce overhead compared to static code. Efficient use of TRttiContext is critical: contexts should be created once and reused, as repeated creation involves costly internal initializations. Caching discovered metadata such as property lists and method references further optimizes repeated reflection tasks.

The flexibility unlocked by Delphi's RTTI and reflection extends to numerous advanced scenarios:

- Adaptive user interfaces that bind dynamically to data models without precompiled bindings.

- Custom ORM layers that map object properties to database columns automatically, adapting to schema evolution.

- Cross-language interop through metadata-driven marshaling and method invocation.

- Test automation frameworks that discover and run tests based on attributes and method signatures.

Delphi's RTTI acts as both an enabler and catalyst for dynamic programming techniques, permitting solutions that adapt fluidly at runtime. Mastering RTTI unlocks a powerful dimension beyond traditional static typing, providing the foundation for sophisticated frameworks, tooling, and runtime adaptability in complex software systems.

Chapter 3

Component-Based Application Development

In Delphi, building applications is elevated by a powerful component-based architecture that brings visual development, reusability, and rapid deployment to life. This chapter reveals the essential principles and inner workings behind component design, customization, serialization, and advanced interface programming. Master the art of crafting scalable, maintainable Delphi applications with components as your creative building blocks.

3.1. Component Design Principles

The effective design of software components hinges on the dual objectives of reusability and robustness, applicable across both design-time and runtime environments. Achieving these goals requires a careful balance between abstraction, flexibility, lifecycle management, and user interaction through property customization. This section delves into key principles that underpin the creation of such components.

Fundamentals of Reusability and Robustness

Reusable components must be designed with clear, well-defined interfaces that encapsulate implementation details while exposing only the necessary functionality. Encapsulation ensures that components can be integrated into diverse contexts without unintended side effects or dependency conflicts. Interfaces should be minimized to those essential for interaction, limiting coupling and promoting adaptability.

Robustness demands that components handle erroneous inputs and exceptional conditions gracefully at runtime, without compromising overall system stability. Defensive programming techniques, including input validation and error reporting, are critical. Additionally, components should be thread-safe if intended for concurrent environments, requiring synchronization strategies or immutable state designs to prevent race conditions.

Lifecycle Management

Lifecycle management orchestrates the initialization, usage, and disposal phases of a component, fostering predictable and reliable behavior. A component's lifecycle typically encompasses:

- **Instantiation**: Establishing internal state and allocating necessary resources.

- **Initialization**: Configuring properties and preparing for runtime operations.

- **Activation**: Transition to an operational state where the component performs its intended functionality.

- **Deactivation or Disposal**: Releasing resources, terminating ongoing activities, and detaching from the hosting environment.

Implementing explicit lifecycle methods, such as `Initialize()`, `Start()`, and `Dispose()`, allows the host environment or the component user to manage state transitions reliably. The use of standardized lifecycle interfaces or base classes can facilitate consistent management and integration, especially in complex frameworks.

Automatic resource management patterns such as the *Disposable* pattern or the RAII (Resource Acquisition Is Initialization) idiom help prevent resource leaks and ensure timely cleanup. Incorporating event hooks or callbacks at various lifecycle stages further enhances flexibility, allowing extendable behavior without subclassing or invasive modifications.

Custom Property Editors

Design-time support greatly enhances developer productivity and component usability by offering intuitive, context-sensitive property editing. Custom property editors provide specialized user interfaces for configuring component properties beyond the default type editors.

Creating custom property editors involves defining editors that can handle complex property types, enforce validation rules, and offer constrained value selections. For example, a color property may be edited using a color picker dialog rather than textual input, reducing the likelihood of invalid values and improving user experience.

Integration with component development environments necessitates adherence to established editor interfaces or design-time metadata specifications. These typically involve:

- Implementing editor classes that extend base property editor frameworks.

- Associating editors with component properties via attribute metadata.

- Supporting serialization and undo-redo mechanisms within the design environment.

Custom editors not only accelerate design-time configuration but also encourage correct use by exposing only valid options, providing real-time feedback, and preventing misconfiguration.

Maximizing Component Flexibility

Flexibility is essential for components to be reusable across multiple scenarios and adaptable to evolving requirements. Key strategies include:

- **Parameterization**: Allowing comprehensive yet controlled configuration through properties, method parameters, and constructor arguments enables tailored behavior without code modification.

- **Extensibility**: Supporting subclassing or composition patterns enables users to extend or replace functionality. Favoring composition over inheritance reduces coupling and improves maintainability.

- **Decoupling**: Designing components to minimize dependencies on environment specifics or other components ensures portability and ease of integration.

- **Event-driven Architectures**: Providing event hooks or callback interfaces allows clients to inject custom behavior asynchronously or react to component state changes.

- **Interface-based Contracts**: Defining strict interface contracts over concrete class usage allows alternative implementations and simplifies testing.

Implementing these strategies often requires judicious use of design patterns such as Strategy, Observer, and Decorator, which encourage separation of concerns and modular design.

Ensuring Component Reliability

Reliable components must perform consistently under a variety of conditions and must be tolerant of faults. Several principles contribute to this objective:

- **Validation and Verification**: Validating all input parameters at the earliest point prevents propagation of errors. Precondition checks and invariants should be explicitly defined.

- **Error Handling and Reporting**: Components must catch anticipated exceptions and either handle them internally or propagate meaningful error messages upstream. Logging mechanisms facilitate debugging and post-mortem analysis.

- **Idempotency**: Designing operations to be idempotent where feasible mitigates side effects from retries or repeated invocations.

- **Concurrency Control**: Synchronization is vital when components operate in multi-threaded environments, ensuring data consistency and avoiding deadlocks or race conditions.

- **Testing and Validation**: Automated unit tests, integration tests, and stress tests should be developed to verify component behavior against specification.

Robust components often embed internal diagnostics and self-tests, enabling early detection of corruption or misconfiguration during their lifecycle.

Illustrative Example: Lifecycle and Property Editor Integration

Consider a graphical UI component designed for a design-time environment:

```
public class CustomButton extends UIComponent implements
    Disposable {
    private Color backgroundColor;

    public void initialize() {
        // Allocate resources or set initial state
        this.backgroundColor = Color.WHITE;
    }

    public void start() {
        // Activate behavior, register event listeners
        enableRendering();
    }

    public void dispose() {
        // Cleanup resources and unregister listeners
        disableRendering();
    }

    public Color getBackgroundColor() {
        return backgroundColor;
    }

    public void setBackgroundColor(Color color) {
        if (color == null) throw new IllegalArgumentException("
    Color cannot be null");
        this.backgroundColor = color;
        refreshDisplay();
    }
}

// Custom property editor for the backgroundColor property
public class ColorPickerEditor extends PropertyEditor {
    @Override
    public Component getEditorComponent() {
        // Returns a color picker UI component for design time
        return new ColorPickerDialog();
    }
}
```

This example illustrates a clear separation of lifecycle phases with explicit resource management and simple validation in setters. The integration of a custom property editor enhances the design-time setup by presenting a graphical color picker rather than raw text input, thereby enforcing correctness and improving usability.

Adhering to these foundational principles contributes to the development of components that are not only reusable and robust but also provide a superior user and developer experience throughout their lifecycle. The synergy between disciplined lifecycle management, custom property editing, and flexible, reliable design patterns forms the cornerstone of modern component-based software engineering.

3.2. VCL Architecture and Customization

The Visual Component Library (VCL) serves as a comprehensive framework that abstracts Windows API complexities, facilitating rapid application development through a rich set of visual and non-visual components. Its design embraces object-oriented principles, enabling extensive customization, extensibility, and event-driven programming. Understanding the VCL architecture requires a detailed analysis of three primary aspects: its event model, visual hierarchy, and message handling system. Additionally, customization techniques such as control subclassing, drag-and-drop implementation, and custom message processing are critical for harnessing the full power of the library.

Event Model

At the core of the VCL's responsiveness lies its event model, which employs a delegate-based architecture to bind UI actions to application code. Events in the VCL are essentially properties of method pointers, allowing components to expose standardized callback slots. For instance, a `TButton` exposes the `OnClick` event, which can be assigned to any procedure with a signature matching `TNotifyEvent`. This delegate encapsulation decouples event sources from handlers, promoting modular design.

When an event is triggered, the component invokes the assigned handler method directly, bypassing the need for explicit Windows

59

message decoding by the developer in most cases. Event propagation follows the principle of immediate execution; the event handler runs synchronously within the context of the calling thread. This straightforward mechanism simplifies interaction patterns compared to raw message handling.

Visual Hierarchy

The VCL adopts a parent-child model to manage the visual composition of components. Controls derive from TWinControl, an abstract class representing windowed controls that allocate Windows handles. Non-windowed controls extend TGraphicControl and rely on their parent window for painting and message processing.

Each TWinControl can contain multiple child controls, forming an explicit tree structure where the Parent property links children to hosts. This hierarchy impacts Z-ordering, coordinate translation, paint invalidation, and message routing. The framework automatically manages these interactions to maintain visual coherence and ensure efficient redrawing.

Coordinate systems are localized: each child control's Left and Top properties are relative to its parent's client area origin. This allows recursive computations of absolute positions when handling low-level messages or implementing complex layouts.

Extensibility and Control Customization

The VCL architecture facilitates seamless control customization through subclassing and method overriding. The fundamental design leverages virtual methods such as Paint, CreateWnd, and WndProc to allow component developers to intercept and augment native behaviors.

Overriding WndProc for Message Hooking

The WndProc method acts as the central dispatcher for Windows messages to a control. Overriding this method enables developers to intercept messages before or after default processing. For example, custom behaviors, such as handling additional messages or modifying paint operations, can be injected here.

```
type
  TMyCustomControl = class(TWinControl)
  protected
    procedure WndProc(var Message: TMessage); override;
  end;

procedure TMyCustomControl.WndProc(var Message: TMessage);
begin
  case Message.Msg of
    WM_LBUTTONDOWN:
      begin
        // Implement custom left-click handling
        HandleCustomClick;
        Message.Result := 0;
        Exit; // Prevent default processing
      end;
  end;
  inherited WndProc(Message);
end;
```

Painting and Appearance Customization

Custom painting is achieved by overriding the Paint method, used primarily by TGraphicControl descendants or windowed controls after their WM_PAINT is processed. Using the Canvas property grants device context access for GDI drawing operations, enabling complex visual effects.

Runtime Property Alterations

VCL controls support dynamic property adjustment, often triggering behavior changes or visual refreshes. Developers can introduce new properties by subclassing and registering them through Delphi's type system, enabling design-time and runtime configurability.

Implementing Drag-and-Drop

VCL abstracts drag-and-drop through a system of event handlers and helper methods built on top of Windows OLE drag-and-drop

61

API. The necessary components include:

- Initiation of dragging via `BeginDrag` or programmatic invocation of drag managers.

- Handling `OnStartDrag`, `OnDragOver`, and `OnDrop` events to manage data transfer and feedback.

- Using `TDragObject` or custom descendant classes to encapsulate drag information and logic.

Proper use requires synchronizing drag source and target controls, along with data format negotiation when crossing application boundaries.

```
procedure TSourceControl.OnMouseDown(Sender: TObject; Button:
    TMouseButton;
  Shift: TShiftState; X, Y: Integer);
begin
  if Button = mbLeft then
    BeginDrag(False);
end;

procedure TTargetControl.OnDragOver(Sender, Source: TObject; X, Y
    : Integer;
  State: TDragState; var Accept: Boolean);
begin
  Accept := Source is TSourceControl;
end;

procedure TTargetControl.OnDragDrop(Sender, Source: TObject; X, Y
    : Integer);
begin
  // Process drop data or perform operations
  HandleDrop(TSourceControl(Source));
end;
```

Efficient Handling of Custom Messages

While the VCL shields most interactions from explicit Windows API message management, complex applications often require custom message handling for inter-component communication or extended functionality. The recommended approach involves defining user messages using constants above `WM_USER`:

$$\text{const} \quad MY\_CUSTOM\_MSG = WM\_USER + 100;$$

Custom messages are sent via `PostMessage` or `SendMessage` to the control's handle and processed in an overridden `WndProc`:

```
procedure TMyControl.WndProc(var Message: TMessage);
begin
  if Message.Msg = MY_CUSTOM_MSG then
  begin
    // Handle the custom operation
    PerformCustomAction(Message.WParam, Message.LParam);
    Message.Result := 0;
  end else
    inherited WndProc(Message);
end;
```

This pattern preserves default message handling while allowing fine-grained control over application-specific protocols. Additionally, the VCL defines `CM_` custom message constants for internal framework notifications, which can be harnessed or extended by developers for consistent integration.

The VCL encourages leveraging inheritance and composition to build sophisticated controls while maintaining compatibility with Windows native behavior. Its event-driven model maps well onto typical GUI requirements, and the visual hierarchy ensures intuitive coordinate management and painting behavior. By understanding and applying methods such as `WndProc` overriding, event binding, and standardized drag-and-drop interfaces, developers can implement rich, responsive, and extensible applications. Custom message handling further enables inter-component coordination beyond ordinary event callbacks, forming a flexible backbone for advanced VCL-based systems.

3.3. FireMonkey (FMX) Framework Internals

The FireMonkey (FMX) framework is a comprehensive cross-platform visual application framework designed to deliver rich, high-performance graphical interfaces across diverse operating systems, including Windows, macOS, iOS, and Android. At its core, FMX abstracts platform-specific UI components and rendering technologies to enable developers to create visually sophisticated applications with a unified codebase. This capability hinges on tightly integrated subsystems that manage styling, 2D and 3D graphics processing, and advanced visual effects.

FMX's internal architecture is founded on a layered rendering pipeline optimized to interchangeably support platform-native APIs such as Direct2D/Direct3D on Windows, Metal on macOS and iOS, and OpenGL or Vulkan on other platforms. The framework encapsulates these disparate APIs behind a common GPU-accelerated canvas, promoting hardware-accelerated rendering and smooth animations regardless of the underlying OS. A key attribute is the use of vector graphics primitives rather than pixel-based bitmaps, enabling resolution-independent drawing that scales gracefully on varying device form factors.

The rendering pipeline processes visual elements as *TCanvas*-based drawing commands. Custom controls and built-in components invoke these commands, which FMX then translates into GPU instructions via its multi-API backend. This ensures that geometric shapes, paths, text layouts, gradients, and bitmap shaders are rendered efficiently in hardware-accelerated contexts. The abstraction extends beyond simple shapes to support 3D scene graphs, compositing, and resource management.

Custom styling in FMX is achieved through an extensible style system that decouples component logic from presentation. Style definitions reside in XML-based .style files, which describe control templates using a hierarchy of style objects, effects, and visual states. Each control maps to one or more style templates, allowing dynamic application of customized appearances.

Internally, FMX loads these styles into *TStyleBook* components, which can be assigned at design time or runtime to form-wide or application-wide containers. The framework's style engine interprets these style descriptions, instantiates visual elements corresponding to styled parts, and manages state transitions such as hover, pressed, or disabled states via visual state managers.

This system supports the application of third-party or user-defined look and feel without modifying control internals. Beyond simple color or font changes, styling can redefine control structure by replacing internal visual subcomponents with complex objects (e.g., animated brushes, path effects), facilitating highly customizable user interfaces. Incorporating style animation and resource references within styles further amplifies the potential for dynamic and responsive designs.

The FMX framework uniquely blends 2D user interface elements with 3D graphics, providing a unified visual experience. The 3D engine is tightly integrated into the same rendering pipeline, supporting scene graphs composed of meshes, materials, lights, and cameras. Developers use *TViewport3D* to embed 3D scenes within an otherwise 2D UI, enabling layered and interactive visualizations.

Internally, FMX's 3D layer utilizes a retained mode rendering system where geometric data and scene graph nodes are stored in memory and efficiently transmitted to the GPU each frame. Materials support complex shading models, including lighting and texture mapping, via programmable shaders abstracted through FMX materials and effects classes. This design allows seamless blending of 3D visuals with 2D controls, facilitating overlays, embedded controls on 3D objects, and advanced composition.

Resource management is a critical internal concern, with FMX managing GPU assets such as vertex buffers, textures, and shader programs. Optimization techniques include culling, batching, and state synchronization with the underlying graphics API to maximize frame rates and maintain responsiveness.

FMX's visual richness is further enhanced by a modular

system of built-in effects that operate on *TBitmap* buffers or directly within the rendering pipeline. These include blur, glow, shadows, reflections, and morphing effects, implemented through GPU-accelerated shaders or image processing algorithms. Effects can be chained and composed, allowing complex visual transformations to be achieved declaratively.

The effects framework integrates closely with the style system, where effects can be embedded in styles and animated in response to user interactions or application state changes. Underlying this capability, FMX maintains a graph of effect nodes that process rendering targets in real-time, exploiting the GPU's programmable pipeline for efficient computation.

Beyond static effects, FMX supports animation frameworks that interpolate property values over time, enabling smooth transitions and transformations. The framework's tight coupling between animation, styling, and effects promotes highly dynamic interfaces without sacrificing performance.

A fundamental challenge FMX addresses is rendering consistent and performant visuals across operating systems with different graphical subsystems and hardware constraints. FMX employs platform adaptation layers that translate common visual idioms into platform-appropriate implementations while preserving behavior and appearance.

The framework leverages conditional style loading, platform-specific resources, and input event normalization to ensure controls respond and render correctly. GPU abstraction layers handle feature discrepancies by falling back to software rendering or simplified effects when necessary. Furthermore, FMX incorporates DPI-aware scaling and input mapping to cater to the diverse device capabilities and screen densities encountered in mobile and desktop environments.

Internally, the modular design facilitates the extension of rendering backends and input systems, which is essential for maintaining forward compatibility with evolving operating system APIs. This adaptability ensures that applications built on FMX benefit from native hardware acceleration and system-level optimizations without sacrificing portability or requiring platform-specific code.

The interplay between FMX's rendering pipeline, style system, 2D/3D integration, and effects constitutes a robust architecture designed for flexibility and scalability. Controls render via styles that define visual structures and effects, which in turn invoke GPU-accelerated drawing on canvases unified across platforms. The 3D scene graph seamlessly interleaves with 2D UI elements, backed by sophisticated resource and state management systems. Animations and effects operate within this integrated environment to enrich user experiences. This internal synergy empowers developers to build visually compelling, high-performance applications that maintain consistent aesthetics and behaviors regardless of underlying platform disparities.

3.4. Component Serialization and Persistence

Serialization of software components is a fundamental mechanism enabling the capture and restoration of component state, facilitating persistent storage, network transmission, and runtime state migration. Unlike simple data structures, components often encapsulate complex state, transient connections, and intricate lifecycle dependencies, requiring sophisticated serialization strategies beyond straightforward byte streams. The process of component serialization thus hinges on a careful orchestration of custom readers and writers, rigorous state versioning, and lifecycle-aware persistence that maintains fidelity and robustness throughout the component's existence.

At the core of component serialization lies the concept of *streaming*—the transformation of an in-memory component representation into a linear sequence of bytes, and its corresponding reconstitution. Simple serialization techniques, such as shallow copying of public fields, are inadequate for stateful components since internal invariants, contextual pointers, and non-serializable members must be handled explicitly. Custom writers and readers thus become indispensable. A *custom writer* is responsible for encoding only the semantically relevant state attributes into the output stream, omitting volatile or easily reconstructable data, while a *custom reader* must reconstruct the component's state from the serialized format, often invoking initialization sequences to reestablish valid state.

Custom serialization logic typically involves overriding or extending generalized serialization interfaces. For example, methods such as `writeObject` and `readObject` in Java, or analogous hooks in C++ or .NET, allow selective field serialization and insertion of consistency checks during reading and writing. It is crucial that custom writers explicitly document serialized fields, allowing for transparent, maintainable, and debuggable persistence.

A representative pattern for custom serialization can be outlined in pseudocode as follows:

```
private void writeObject(ObjectOutputStream out) throws
    IOException {
    // Serialize the version number for future compatibility
    out.writeInt(CURRENT_VERSION);
    // Serialize fields explicitly
    out.writeUTF(componentName);
    out.writeInt(stateValue);
    // Serialize complex objects recursively or with their own
     serialization
    nestedComponent.writeObject(out);
}

private void readObject(ObjectInputStream in) throws IOException,
    ClassNotFoundException {
    int version = in.readInt();
    // Version-dependent reading
    if(version == 1) {
        componentName = in.readUTF();
        stateValue = in.readInt();
        nestedComponent = new NestedComponent();
        nestedComponent.readObject(in);
```

```
    } else {
        // Handle other versions or throw an exception
        throw new IOException("Unsupported version: " + version);
    }
    // Reinitialize transient fields
    initializeTransients();
}
```

The incorporation of a *versioning scheme* is imperative for maintaining compatibility across component evolution. Components inevitably undergo state schema changes—field additions, removals, or type modifications. Without a proper versioning mechanism, serialized data becomes stale or incompatible, endangering data integrity and system stability. A robust versioning strategy involves embedding metadata such as version numbers or schema identifiers within the serialized stream and employing conditional logic during deserialization to adaptively process state conforming to various versions.

More sophisticated systems use semantic versioning with optional forward and backward compatibility guarantees, employing techniques such as default values for missing fields, graceful ignoring of unknown fields, or migration hooks that transform older state representations into current formats. Employing schema definition languages (e.g., Protocol Buffers, Avro) or component-specific serialization formats further strengthens version control by enforcing explicit, machine-parseable schema descriptions.

Persistence of component state must also gracefully integrate with the component lifecycle. Components frequently have transient resources such as open network connections, file handles, or computational caches that are inappropriate for serialization. Lifecycle management requires carefully suspending, saving, and restoring such resources without violating system constraints or causing resource leaks. To ensure seamless lifecycle management:

- **Pre-serialization hooks** should quiesce volatile state, flush buffers, and suspend activities.

- **Post-deserialization hooks** must reestablish connections, reinitialize caches, and reattach listeners.

- **Transactional semantics** for serialization operations protect against partial or failed persistence attempts, maintaining component consistency.

For example, a typical lifecycle-aware persistence pattern includes explicit `prepareForSerialization()` and `restoreAfterDeserialization()` methods invoked during the serialization cycle:

```
public void prepareForSerialization() {
    // Close or flush transient resources
    connection.close();
    cache.clear();
}

public void restoreAfterDeserialization() {
    // Reinitialize transient resources
    connection = connectionFactory.open();
    cache = new ComponentCache();
}
```

Integrating such lifecycle hooks requires discipline, usually enforced by design contracts or base component abstractions.

Beyond individual components, component serialization must address composite and hierarchical structures. Composite components often contain nested subcomponents, each with its own state and lifecycle. Recursive serialization methods must carefully serialize the entire graph of component dependencies, ensuring proper ordering, cycle detection, and identity preservation when multiple references to the same component exist. Data models like graphs or trees within components can utilize reference tables or object identifiers to avoid duplication and maintain referential integrity.

Finally, component serialization strategies should align with performance and security considerations. Serialization cost includes CPU overhead, memory footprint, and I/O latency; efficient binary formats or incremental serialization approaches mitigate these overheads. From a security standpoint, untrusted serialization data can compromise component integrity or trigger denial of service; thus, input validation, restricting permissible types, and defensive deserialization are necessary safeguards.

In sum, effective component serialization and persistence demands a comprehensive framework combining custom streaming logic, explicit versioning, lifecycle synchronization, and careful management of nested dependencies. Mastery of these concepts empowers precise control over component state management, fostering robust, adaptable, and maintainable software systems.

3.5. Event-Driven Programming Model

The event-driven programming model is foundational in Delphi for creating applications capable of responsive interaction and scalable asynchronous processing. Its architectural significance arises from the central role of *events* and *delegates* (method pointers) in decoupling components and enabling reactive behavior across diverse runtime scenarios.

In Delphi, *events* represent abstractions of occurrences or state changes within a system, which may stem from user gestures, system notifications, or internal application signals. These events are encapsulated as properties typed as procedural method pointers, formally known as *event handlers*. A delegate is a strongly typed reference to a class method that acts as a callback, enabling the invocation of code in response to an event without creating rigid dependencies between the event source and the event consumer.

At the core of the model lies the architecture of event declaration and handling. Events are typically declared as property types of the form:

```
type
  TNotifyEvent = procedure(Sender: TObject) of object;
```

```
TButton = class
private
  FOnClick: TNotifyEvent;
public
  property OnClick: TNotifyEvent read FOnClick write FOnClick;
  procedure Click;
end;
```

The TNotifyEvent type defines a delegate for methods with a Sender parameter indicating the source. The OnClick property exposes this delegate. The Click method triggers the event:

```
procedure TButton.Click;
begin
  if Assigned(FOnClick) then
    FOnClick(Self);
end;
```

This pattern ensures that any consumer of the TButton component can subscribe to the OnClick event by assigning procedure references that match the delegate's signature. Importantly, the sender parameter enables contextual information to be passed without tight coupling.

Delphi's event model naturally supports asynchronous operations by allowing the event triggers to be invoked in different execution contexts. For instance, non-blocking I/O or timer-based events can perform work on background threads or message loops and deliver notifications back to the main thread via events. The use of delegates allows seamless invocation of event handlers regardless of the underlying concurrency mechanism. This design supports scalable architectures such as asynchronous UI updates or network message processing while maintaining thread safety through synchronization mechanisms.

Crafting *custom events* extends the flexibility inherent in Delphi's event architecture. Developers may define unique event signatures tailored to specific application semantics. For example, an event signaling a progress update might be declared as:

```
type
```

```
TProgressEvent = procedure(Sender: TObject; PercentDone:
   Integer) of object;

TDownloader = class
private
  FOnProgress: TProgressEvent;
public
   property OnProgress: TProgressEvent read FOnProgress write
   FOnProgress;
   procedure Download;
end;
```

In this paradigm, the Download procedure might trigger events with various progress values, invoking subscribed handlers with precise, application-specific state data. The delegate type ensures strict typing while maintaining the flexibility to propagate rich event information.

Reactive programming models in Delphi increasingly employ these event and delegate constructs to create *reactive streams* of events. By composing observable sequences and registering callback delegates, applications achieve responsive, event-driven architectures that react to asynchronous data flows and user interactions without imperative polling or tightly coupled state management.

A fundamental reactive pattern involves chaining event transformations and side effects, promoting separation of concerns and enabling declarative handling of asynchronous behavior. This architectural style aligns closely with Delphi's visual component and event model paradigms but extends beyond UI-centric usage to network communication, data streams, and concurrent processing.

For example, constructing a reactive pipeline might involve:

- Defining a delegate type capturing specific event data.

- Creating a component that exposes events triggering on conditional states.

- Subscribing to these events with handlers implementing transformation or forwarding logic.

This approach encourages loose coupling between producers and consumers of events, which is indispensable in large-scale, modular applications requiring high maintainability and adaptability.

In summary, the architectural significance of events and delegates in Delphi is multifaceted. They serve as the primary mechanism for asynchronous operation, callback management, and reactive programming integration. Mastery of event declaration patterns, delegate assignment, and event invocation strategies underpins the development of scalable and responsive applications. Custom event design allows for domain-specific, context-rich signaling, while embracing reactive programming models fosters a clean, maintainable approach to complex, dynamic application logic.

The seamless integration of events and delegates within Delphi's type system, UI framework, and runtime infrastructure makes the event-driven programming model an indispensable skillset for architects and developers targeting efficient, robust software solutions.

3.6. Theming, Styling, and Accessibility

Designing applications that seamlessly adapt to diverse user preferences and system-wide visual requirements demands a sophisticated approach to theming, styling, and accessibility. At an advanced level, the objective transcends basic UI customization; it requires the creation of interfaces that are both flexible and inherently accessible, ensuring inclusivity without compromising aesthetic or functional coherence.

Dynamic theming architectures begin with a flexible architecture capable of responding dynamically to user settings and contextual cues. Central to this is the abstraction of stylistic variables—colors,

74

typography, spacing, and iconography—into a coherent theme model. Utilizing design tokens, defined as platform-agnostic variables representing core design attributes, enables consistent application of styles and facilitates global updates.

Dynamic theming can be driven by two complementary inputs: explicit user preferences and system cues such as dark mode or high-contrast modes. Theming engines must implement a priority hierarchy to reconcile these inputs, often layering user overrides atop system defaults. This layering necessitates a state management approach where theme states are encapsulated in immutable objects or context providers, enabling efficient propagation of style changes without redundant recalculations or re-renders.

An example implementation pattern involves encapsulating theme tokens within a context:

```
import React, { createContext, useContext, useState } from 'react';

const ThemeContext = createContext();

export function ThemeProvider({ children }) {
  const [theme, setTheme] = useState(defaultTheme);

  const toggleDarkMode = () => {
    setTheme(current => current.mode === 'dark' ? defaultTheme :
    darkTheme);
  };

  return (
    <ThemeContext.Provider value={{ theme, toggleDarkMode }}>
      {children}
    </ThemeContext.Provider>
  );
}

export function useTheme() {
  return useContext(ThemeContext);
}
```

This pattern ensures centralized theme control, facilitating synchronization of style across complex, componentized applications.

Styling for accessibility and contrast imposes rigorous constraints on styling choices. Foremost among these is the need for sufficient contrast ratios to accommodate users with visual impairments, particularly those with low vision or color blindness. WCAG 2.1 guidelines prescribe distinct minimum contrast ratios: 4.5:1 for normal text and 3:1 for larger text.

Automated contrast verification tools can be integrated into the development pipeline, but advanced applications proactively adapt their styles in real-time. This often involves generating accessible color palettes programmatically rather than relying on static color swatches. Techniques such as luminance adjustment and hue rotation can adjust colors dynamically to maintain contrast without disrupting brand identity.

For instance, a luminance scaling function can be formulated mathematically as

$$L_{\text{new}} = \begin{cases} L \times (1 + \alpha), & \text{if } L \leq 0.5 \\ L \times (1 - \alpha), & \text{if } L > 0.5 \end{cases}$$

where L is the original luminance value (normalized between 0 and 1) and α is a scaling coefficient tuned to improve contrast.

Furthermore, styling must accommodate semantic HTML elements and ARIA roles, ensuring that visual presentation corresponds logically to accessible structure. CSS should avoid purely visual indicators such as color alone to convey critical information; instead, it should supplement with textual cues or icons accessible by screen readers.

User adaptability extends beyond color schemes. Advanced systems implement multiple axes of customization to tailor interfaces to individual needs. Examples include font size scaling, spacing adjustments, and alternative input modalities support, such as keyboard navigation or voice control.

Implementing these features requires exposing a user preferences interface with persistence at either client or server side. Preferences can conform to standardized specifications—such as the CSS Media Queries Level 5 specification that includes `prefers-reduced-motion` and `prefers-contrast`—which inform default style adaptations.

Custom controls must themselves be thoroughly accessible and themable. This involves designing components that respond to focus states, support high contrast themes, and maintain operability under assistive technologies. For example, focus outlines should be preserved or enhanced rather than removed, and interactive area sizes must meet minimum touch-target dimensions (44 by 44 pixels according to Microsoft's accessibility guidelines).

Integration with system APIs where available can further enhance adaptation. For instance, macOS and Windows provide system-initiated accessibility settings that applications can query and respond to, augmenting the theming system with richer environmental context.

A critical technical challenge lies in ensuring consistent theming and accessibility across multiple platforms and application states. Design tokens must be carefully managed through versioning and scoping to prevent regression or conflicts. The use of atomic CSS or utility-first style frameworks can provide deterministic styling, but they must be augmented with theme-aware design patterns.

State-based styling patterns—such as hover, focus, active, and disabled—require both visual clarity and accessibility compliance. A focus on feature queries in CSS enables conditional styling based on environment capabilities, improving resilience to varied user agents and assistive technology implementations.

Testing strategies also require sophistication. Unit and integration tests should incorporate automated accessibility audits (e.g., axe-core, Lighthouse), while visual regression testing must validate theming continuity after code changes. User testing, especially with individuals who utilize assistive technologies, provides irreplaceable insights into real-world theming and accessibility behavior.

Ultimately, advanced theming, styling, and accessibility are inseparable facets of a single design imperative: creating user interfaces that are adaptable, inclusive, and maintainable. By employing dynamic theme architectures, programmatic contrast management, extensive customization options, and rigorous testing, development teams can deliver applications that meet both aesthetic aspirations and the diverse needs of their user base. This integrated approach not only ensures compliance with accessibility standards but also elevates the overall user experience across all contexts and modalities.

Chapter 4

Data Access and Multitier Architecture

Effective data access and scalable architecture are at the core of modern Delphi solutions. In this chapter, unlock the advanced frameworks, technologies, and patterns that transform data integration into a robust, maintainable foundation for application growth. Go beyond connectivity—embrace ORM, multitier designs, and performance optimizations to architect Delphi systems that are agile, resilient, and enterprise-ready.

4.1. Advanced FireDAC and dbExpress Usage

Efficient database connectivity is crucial for high-performance backend operations in Delphi applications. FireDAC and dbExpress provide flexible and powerful frameworks for accessing a wide range of databases, but leveraging their advanced features requires a deep understanding of connection pooling, transaction management, and scalability tactics.

Connection Pooling

Connection pooling significantly enhances application responsiveness and resource management by reusing a pool of active database connections rather than creating and destroying connections repeatedly. FireDAC supports internal connection pooling, which can be enabled via the TFDConnection component settings.

The primary parameters to control connection pooling behavior are ConnectionDef and UpdateOptions.PoolSize. For example:

```
FDConnection1.Params.DriverID := 'PG';
FDConnection1.Params.Database := 'MyDB';
FDConnection1.Params.UserName := 'user';
FDConnection1.Params.Password := 'pass';
FDConnection1.Params.Add('Pooled=True');        // Enable pooling
FDConnection1.UpdateOptions.PoolSize := 20;   // Maximum
     connections in pool
FDConnection1.Connected := True;
```

The Pooled=True parameter instructs FireDAC to maintain connections in a pool shared across threads, minimizing the overhead of repeated connection creation. The PoolSize limits the number of connections queued, preventing uncontrolled resource consumption. Note that to maximize scaling across threads, the ResourceOptions.ThreadSafe property should be set to True.

In contrast, dbExpress does not provide native connection pooling; therefore, custom pooling mechanisms or middleware must be employed. This typically involves managing a centralized pool of TSQLConnection instances, synchronized with critical sections or other thread-safe constructs to avoid race conditions.

Complex Transaction Management

Robust transaction control is essential for maintaining data integrity in applications performing multiple, interdependent operations. FireDAC offers comprehensive transaction management through TFDConnection methods such as StartTransaction, Commit, and Rollback. More sophisticated scenarios, such as nested transactions and savepoints, are also supported.

Nested transactions enable partial rollbacks within a broader transaction context. FireDAC implements this via savepoints:

```
FDConnection1.StartTransaction;
try
  // Perform main transaction work
  FDConnection1.StartSavePoint('SP1');
  try
    // Subtask that may fail
    FDConnection1.ExecSQL('UPDATE Table SET Col = ? WHERE ID =
    ?', [NewValue, ID]);
    FDConnection1.CommitSavePoint('SP1');
  except
    // Roll back to savepoint without aborting outer transaction
    FDConnection1.RollbackSavePoint('SP1');
  end;
  FDConnection1.Commit;
except
  FDConnection1.Rollback;
  raise;
end;
```

When using dbExpress, explicit support for nested transactions and savepoints depends on the underlying database driver capabilities. Transaction control is generally limited to basic StartTransaction, Commit, and Rollback calls. It is advisable to incorporate database-specific SQL commands for savepoints within TSQLQuery executions if required.

For long-running or distributed transactions, FireDAC can coordinate with external transaction managers through its support of Microsoft Distributed Transaction Coordinator (DTC) or XA transactions, adding scalability in enterprise environments.

Scalable and Reliable Data Interaction

FireDAC's architecture inherently supports asynchronous execution and multiplexed access, essential for scalable database operations. Setting the ResourceOptions.AsyncMode to amCancelDialog or amNonBlocking permits query execution without blocking UI threads.

81

Batch processing is another critical optimization. FireDAC allows batched updates for datasets through the TFDTable or TFDQuery components by enabling cached updates:

```
FDQuery1.CachedUpdates := True;
// Perform multiple dataset modifications here
FDQuery1.ApplyUpdates(0);  // Commit all changes in a batch
```

Batching reduces network overhead and database round-trips, thus improving throughput, especially over high-latency connections.

Error handling in batch operations requires care. FireDAC provides detailed error reporting mechanisms via the OnReconcileError event, enabling granular resolution of conflicts or constraint violations without aborting the entire batch.

To enhance reliability, configure FireDAC's FetchOptions to optimize data retrieval patterns. For example, setting FetchOptions.Mode to fmOnDemand delays fetching rows until accessed, minimizing initial response times and memory overhead for large datasets.

FireDAC also supports multi-threaded applications by ensuring that all dataset and connection components interacting on different threads operate on independent connection instances, preferably obtained from the connection pool. FireDAC's internal thread safety constructs minimize risks of data corruption or deadlocks.

Compared to FireDAC, dbExpress requires more explicit threading and connection management by the developer. It is necessary to instantiate and configure distinct TSQLConnection and TSQLQuery components per thread, avoiding shared state unless synchronized.

Best Practices Summary

- Enable connection pooling in FireDAC for scalable high-load

82

scenarios; tune `PoolSize` to balance resource constraints and concurrency requirements.

- Utilize savepoints for nested transaction management in FireDAC, enabling partial rollback and enhanced error containment.

- Implement asynchronous query execution and cached updates to reduce UI stalls and improve throughput.

- Ensure thread safety by isolating connections per thread and using FireDAC's internal synchronization features.

- Leverage FireDAC's error events to handle batch update conflicts gracefully.

- For dbExpress, employ custom connection pooling and database-specific savepoint SQL to approximate FireDAC's advanced features.

Mastering these advanced techniques maximizes database interaction efficiency and reliability, allowing Delphi applications to scale and respond dynamically under demanding workloads. FireDAC's rich feature set markedly simplifies these tasks relative to dbExpress, but both require thoughtful architecture and rigorous coding disciplines to achieve optimal performance in enterprise-grade software systems.

4.2. Object-Relational Mapping and Entity Frameworks

Object-Relational Mapping (ORM) addresses the fundamental challenge of bridging the conceptual gap between object-oriented programming languages and relational database systems. In Delphi, ORM frameworks facilitate the automatic synchronization of Delphi objects with database tables, dramatically simplifying data access and manipulation. The primary goal is to abstract SQL code, allowing developers to work with objects while the framework handles data persistence.

Delphi ORM frameworks, such as `TMS Aurelius`, `EntityDAC`, and `InstantObjects`, provide comprehensive mechanisms for mapping classes to database tables, properties to columns, and managing associations such as one-to-one, one-to-many, and many-to-many relationships. This automated translation improves maintainability and reduces boilerplate data access code.

Custom mapping strategies play a pivotal role in tailoring the ORM framework to specific application requirements. Mapping can be defined using a variety of approaches:

- **Attribute-Based Mapping:** Declares metadata directly in the Delphi class source code using attributes. This method is type-safe and tightly couples the mapping with the class definition.

- **XML or External Configuration:** Separates mapping metadata from code, enabling dynamic adjustments without recompiling the application.

- **Fluent API Mapping:** Employs method chaining in code to define mappings programmatically, offering flexibility and readability.

Consider a Delphi entity class representing a customer record:

```
type
  [Entity]
  [Table('CUSTOMERS')]
  TCustomer = class
  private
    FId: Integer;
    FName: string;
    FOrders: TObjectList<TOrder>;
  public
    [Column('ID', [TColumnProp.Unique, TColumnProp.Required])]
    property Id: Integer read FId write FId;
```

```
  [Column('NAME', [TColumnProp.Required])]
  property Name: string read FName write FName;

  [Association([TAssociationProp.Lazy], CascadeTypeAll)]
  property Orders: TObjectList<TOrder> read FOrders write
  FOrders;

  constructor Create;
  destructor Destroy; override;
end;
```

The above class illustrates declarative mapping using attributes, specifying table and column names, constraints, and associations. The ORM framework uses this metadata to generate SQL queries and manage object state transitions.

Entity management extends beyond simple CRUD operations. An important concept is the *entity lifecycle,* which includes states such as *transient, persistent, detached,* and *removed.* Effective management of these states is essential for ensuring data integrity and minimizing unnecessary database calls. ORM frameworks typically provide a UnitOfWork or EntityManager component responsible for tracking entity changes:

- **Transient:** Newly created objects not yet persisted.

- **Persistent:** Objects currently tracked and synchronized with the database.

- **Detached:** Previously persistent objects not currently tracked.

- **Removed:** Objects marked for deletion.

The UnitOfWork pattern aggregates changes to multiple entities, efficiently batching updates during a single transaction:

```
var
  UoW: TUow;
  Customer: TCustomer;
begin
```

```
UoW := TUow.Create(Connection);
try
  Customer := TCustomer.Create;
  Customer.Name := 'ACME Corp';
  UoW.Persist(Customer);  // Marks as persistent and schedules
    insert

  // Perform other modifications...

  UoW.Commit;             // Executes all pending SQL in a
    single transaction
finally
  UoW.Free;
end;
end;
```

The separation between business logic and data access is crucial in designing scalable Delphi applications. Employing layered architectures allows developers to isolate entity definitions and persistence mechanisms from the application's core functionality. The business layer encapsulates domain rules and workflows, while the data access layer focuses exclusively on communication with the database via the ORM.

An effective pattern is the *Repository*, which provides a collection-like interface for accessing aggregate roots. A repository shields clients from the complexities of different data sources and promotes testability by enabling mock implementations.

```
type
  ICustomerRepository = interface
    procedure Add(const ACust: TCustomer);
    procedure Remove(const ACust: TCustomer);
    function FindById(const AId: Integer): TCustomer;
    function FindByName(const AName: string): TObjectList<
      TCustomer>;
  end;
```

Implementation of this interface leverages the ORM's entity manager to execute queries and manage object states. This abstraction simplifies business rules, allowing services to operate on domain entities without needing SQL or ORM-specific details.

Sophisticated data access layers crafted with ORM facilitate advanced scenarios including:

- **Lazy Loading:** Defers loading of associated entities until explicitly accessed, optimizing performance.

- **Eager Loading:** Preloads related data to reduce roundtrips.

- **Caching:** Improves response times by reducing database access for frequently requested entities.

- **Inheritance Mapping:** Supports polymorphic behavior by mapping class hierarchies to relational tables using strategies like table-per-class or single-table inheritance.

The use of ORM frameworks within Delphi promotes a consistent and maintainable approach to managing persistent data. By leveraging custom mapping strategies and structured entity management, developers can build robust business and data access layers that reduce boilerplate code, enhance testability, and improve the agility of enterprise applications.

4.3. Multi-tier and DataSnap Architectures

Multi-tier architecture forms the foundation for scalable, maintainable, and distributed application design. By separating concerns across distinct layers-presentation, business logic, and data storage-developers can build systems that are easier to extend and optimize. Delphi's DataSnap framework offers a comprehensive set of tools tailored to implement such architectures with ease, supporting both REST and SOAP protocols for communication. This section explores the methodologies and best practices for architecting scalable multi-tier solutions using DataSnap, emphasizes service-oriented design patterns, and details session management within distributed Delphi applications.

87

At its core, a multi-tier architecture segregates application functionality into layers that may reside on physically separate machines or processes. The traditional three-tier model consists of:

1. **Presentation Tier**: User interface components, usually client applications or web frontends.

2. **Business Logic Tier**: Services encapsulating the core application logic, validation, and workflow.

3. **Data Tier**: Data storage and access mechanisms such as relational databases or other persistent media.

DataSnap enables Delphi developers to build the business logic tier as server modules that expose methods callable by remote clients, thereby enabling distributed applications and services. These DataSnap servers can be implemented using multiple communication protocols-most notably REST and SOAP-which cater to different interoperability and integration needs.

Service orientation is a key principle in multi-tier architectures, promoting loosely coupled, reusable, and interoperable services. DataSnap encourages this through well-defined service interfaces exposed by server methods, which are agnostic to the underlying protocol used for transport.

The *Facade* pattern is prevalent in DataSnap service design. It entails creating a simplified service interface that aggregates multiple backend operations. This encapsulation reduces the complexity exposed to clients and promotes loose coupling between client and server. For example, a server module can expose a single method that internally coordinates calls to several components, providing a unified view of business operations.

Another vital pattern is *Stateless Session Services*. While stateful sessions are supported by DataSnap, especially through session management mechanisms, stateless services facilitate better scalability and load balancing when server instances are distributed

88

across clusters. Statelessness implies that each client request contains all necessary data for processing, eliminating the need for server-side retention of client state.

DataSnap supports RESTful web services, which utilize standard HTTP verbs-GET, POST, PUT, DELETE-and JSON for message encoding. REST is well-suited for web and mobile clients due to its simplicity, wide adoption, and stateless communication style. Configuring a DataSnap server for REST involves defining server methods with appropriate attributes and enabling the REST transport channel.

SOAP, conversely, is a protocol with a formal XML messaging format enveloped in an HTTP or SMTP transport. Despite its verbosity, SOAP excels at enterprise integration scenarios requiring strict contract definitions, policy attachments, and WS-* standards such as WS-Security and transactions. DataSnap's SOAP interface utilizes WSDL to describe services, facilitating interoperability with clients developed using different languages and platforms.

While stateless services are ideal for scalability, many applications require stateful interactions. DataSnap provides session handling mechanisms leveraging a session manager that maintains per-client context data during the lifecycle of a session. Sessions can be identified using cookies, URL parameters, or custom headers depending on client capabilities.

By default, DataSnap sessions are managed on the server side, indexed by unique session identifiers. Developers can store session-specific information in the session's context object to retain user preferences, authentication tokens, or transaction states. However, careful design is required to balance performance and consistency, as excessive state retention can limit scalability and complicate failover scenarios in clustered environments.

To manage sessions, DataSnap exposes four primary lifetime events:

- `OnGetClass`: Initializes server classes dynamically per session.

- `OnGetDSClass`: Creates the server method instances for client interaction.

- `OnPrepareStatement`: Invoked before executing database queries within the service context.

- `OnSessionTerminate`: Allows cleanup logic when a client session ends.

Effective session handling patterns combine server-side context with token-based authentication to ensure both scalability and security.

Successful deployment architecture for DataSnap servers requires a strategy that addresses fault tolerance, scalability, and security. Typically, DataSnap servers are hosted on middleware servers or application servers accessible over the network. They expose endpoints listening for client requests via HTTP, HTTPS, TCP/IP, or named pipes.

Clustering multiple DataSnap instances behind load balancers enables horizontal scaling, distributing client load dynamically. In such setups, stateless services or carefully managed session replication is essential to maintain client context during failover. Load balancers can be hardware appliances or software-based (e.g., reverse proxies, Kubernetes ingress controllers).

Integration with enterprise identity providers and secure transport layers (TLS/SSL) is critical to protect data in transit and authenticate clients. DataSnap servers often integrate with existing Delphi security frameworks such as `TAuthenticationManager` to provide role-based access control, leveraging JSON Web Tokens (JWT) or OAuth2 as external authentication schemes.

To illustrate a basic DataSnap server method definition for REST deployment:

```
type
  TServerMethods1 = class(TDataModule)
  public
    [RESTMethod]
    function GetCustomerName(CustomerID: Integer): string;
  end;

function TServerMethods1.GetCustomerName(CustomerID: Integer):
    string;
begin
  // Business logic to query customer database
  Result := GetNameFromDatabase(CustomerID);
end;
```

The corresponding REST endpoint exposes this method, accessible via HTTP GET, returning JSON-encoded responses compatible with diverse client platforms.

DataSnap's rich support for multi-tier architectures enables Delphi developers to implement scalable, distributed, and interoperable business services. Employing service-oriented patterns, selecting appropriate communication protocols, implementing robust session management, and architecting deployment environments with scalability and security in mind fosters efficient enterprise-grade systems capable of evolving with changing requirements.

4.4. Data Binding and Live Data Feeds

Data binding constitutes a fundamental technique in modern software architecture, enabling synchronization between the underlying data model and the user interface without explicit, imperative code that manipulates UI elements. Declarative data binding leverages this by allowing developers to specify data relationships declaratively, typically through framework-supported syntax, which then automatically manages updates, greatly reducing boilerplate and potential for bugs.

The core abstraction underlying declarative data binding is the *observer pattern*, a design mechanism by which an object, known as the *subject* or *observable*, maintains a list of dependents, called *observers*, and automatically notifies them of any state changes. This pattern decouples the data source from its consumers, fostering modularity and loose coupling across application tiers.

Consider a simple observable object encapsulating state changes:

```java
public class Observable<T> {
    private T value;
    private final List<Observer<T>> observers = new ArrayList<>()
    ;

    public void addObserver(Observer<T> observer) {
        observers.add(observer);
    }

    public void removeObserver(Observer<T> observer) {
        observers.remove(observer);
    }

    public void setValue(T newValue) {
        if (!Objects.equals(value, newValue)) {
            value = newValue;
            notifyObservers();
        }
    }

    public T getValue() {
        return value;
    }

    private void notifyObservers() {
        for (Observer<T> observer : observers) {
            observer.update(value);
        }
    }
}

@FunctionalInterface
public interface Observer<T> {
    void update(T newValue);
}
```

This implementation introduces core elements: a state holder, methods to attach or detach observers, and notification logic triggering updates only upon actual state changes, ensuring efficient propagation. Consumers subscribe by providing update logic encapsulated within the observer interface, enabling loose coupling between data producers and UI components.

Extending from individual observables, complex systems often require *live data feeds*, where streams of data updates propagate through multiple layers-backend services, APIs, middleware, and UI frontends-to provide real-time responsiveness. Architecting such systems demands several architectural considerations:

1. **Event-driven Communication:** Core to live data feeds is the adoption of event-driven paradigms where discrete events representing state changes propagate asynchronously. Message brokers (e.g., Apache Kafka, RabbitMQ) serve as intermediaries to decouple producers from consumers, enabling scalability and reliability.

2. **Push vs. Pull Mechanisms:** Push-based data streaming utilizes protocols like WebSockets or Server-Sent Events to transmit changes initiated by the server, ensuring low-latency updates. Pull-based polling reduces communication overhead but increases client complexity and potential latency.

3. **Data Consistency and Concurrency:** Maintaining consistency across distributed systems requires careful handling of concurrency, eventual consistency models, and conflict resolution strategies, particularly when multiple sources update the same data streams.

4. **State Management and Transformation:** Middleware or client-layer state management frameworks (e.g., Redux or MobX in JavaScript ecosystems) often integrate with live data feeds to maintain an application's state tree, applying transformation and derivation rules declaratively to reflect live data accurately.

Combining declarative data binding with live data feeds is well exemplified in frontend frameworks such as React, Angular, and

Vue.js, which provide built-in mechanisms to bind data models to the Document Object Model (DOM) and automatically update views upon data changes. For example, React's hook system, specifically `useState` and `useEffect`, allows components to respond reactively to live data streams, and frameworks abstract this reactivity, making UI updates declarative and concise.

Architecturally, a robust live data system spans multiple tiers:

- **Data Source Tier:** Sensors, databases, or third-party APIs continually update data.

- **Data Ingestion and Processing Tier:** Streams are ingested and processed, applying filtering, aggregation, or enrichment. Technologies like Apache Flink or Spark Streaming exemplify this tier.

- **API and Middleware Tier:** Serves as the boundary layer exposing data streams to clients through web protocols. Implements authentication, rate limiting, and transformation.

- **Client and Presentation Tier:** Employs data binding frameworks to consume live data streams, updating the interface reactively and efficiently.

A practical example illustrating live data feeds through observer-based binding involves a financial dashboard displaying stock prices that update dynamically in near real-time:

```
// Observable stock price class using callback observers
class StockPrice {
    constructor() {
        this.price = 0;
        this.observers = new Set();
    }

    subscribe(observer) {
        this.observers.add(observer);
    }

    unsubscribe(observer) {
        this.observers.delete(observer);
```

94

```
    }

    setPrice(newPrice) {
        if (this.price !== newPrice) {
            this.price = newPrice;
            this.notify();
        }
    }

    notify() {
        this.observers.forEach((observer) => observer(this.price)
    );
    }
}

const stock = new StockPrice();

stock.subscribe((price) => {
    console.log(`Updated stock price: $${price.toFixed(2)}`);
});

// Simulated live feed updates
setInterval(() => {
    const newPrice = (Math.random() * 1000) + 100;
    stock.setPrice(newPrice);
}, 1000);
```

```
Updated stock price: $745.34
Updated stock price: $872.93
Updated stock price: $1032.75
...
```

This example highlights how the observer pattern supports live updates, ensuring UI elements or downstream logic react automatically when the observed state changes. Extending this approach within a framework context, binding the stock price state to UI components streamlines user interface reactivity without direct DOM manipulation.

Overall, declarative data binding combined with observer-pattern-based live data feeds forms a cornerstone of real-time interactive applications. Architecting such systems requires a comprehensive understanding of data flow mechanisms, concurrency control, and framework-specific reactivity models. Mastery of these concepts empowers the creation of highly responsive, maintainable, and scalable applications that deliver seamless user experiences across diverse platforms and devices.

4.5. SQL Integration and Query Optimization

Integrating complex SQL queries directly within Delphi applications requires a disciplined approach to query construction, execution, and optimization to ensure correctness, high performance, and data integrity under demanding conditions. Central to this integration is the use of parameterized queries, which safeguard against SQL injection, improve execution plan reuse, and maintain clarity when dealing with dynamic query criteria.

Delphi's database components, such as TQuery, TADOQuery, and TFDQuery (FireDAC), provide native support for parameterization. Query parameters should always be used in place of string concatenation to embed variable values. Consider the following exemplary parameterized query using FireDAC:

```
FDQuery1.SQL.Text :=
  'SELECT * FROM Orders WHERE CustomerID = :CustID AND OrderDate
    >= :StartDate';
FDQuery1.ParamByName('CustID').AsString := 'ALFKI';
FDQuery1.ParamByName('StartDate').AsDate := EncodeDate(2023, 1,
    1);
FDQuery1.Open;
```

This method prevents SQL injection by separating variable values from executable code and promotes effective query plan caching by the database engine. Beyond security, parameterization facilitates maintenance and debugging by clearly separating query logic from data.

Query optimization in Delphi involves both SQL tuning and efficient use of the data access components. The essence of SQL tuning lies in minimizing resource-intensive operations such as full table scans, redundant sorting, and excessive data transmission. Conscious use of indexes is the principal lever: crafting queries to exploit existing indexes or creating new ones matching access patterns can drastically reduce execution time.

For instance, filtering on indexed columns rather than applying functional expressions or wrapping columns in functions preserves index utilization. To illustrate:

```
-- Inefficient query, index on OrderDate not used
SELECT * FROM Orders WHERE YEAR(OrderDate) = 2023;

-- Optimized equivalent query using direct range
SELECT * FROM Orders WHERE OrderDate >= '2023-01-01' AND
    OrderDate < '2024-01-01';
```

The latter enables use of an index on `OrderDate` for a range seek operation, significantly improving performance.

Delphi applications benefit from explicit control over transaction scopes, which is critical to ensuring data integrity and consistency, particularly in multi-user or distributed environments. Transactions should encompass logically atomic units of work, demarcated by `StartTransaction`, `Commit`, and `Rollback` calls to protect against partial updates caused by errors or concurrency conflicts:

```
FDConnection1.StartTransaction;
try
  FDQuery1.SQL.Text := 'UPDATE Inventory SET Quantity = Quantity
    - :Qty WHERE ProductID = :ProdID';
  FDQuery1.ParamByName('Qty').AsInteger := 10;
  FDQuery1.ParamByName('ProdID').AsInteger := 123;
  FDQuery1.ExecSQL;
  FDConnection1.Commit;
except
  FDConnection1.Rollback;
  raise;
end;
```

Appropriate transaction management reduces issues such as dirty reads, phantom reads, and lost updates. The isolation level configured via the database or FireDAC properties dictates concurrency control behavior, requiring careful consideration to balance consistency against contention.

Optimizing the amount of data transferred from the database to the application is decisive for responsiveness. Selecting only required columns rather than SELECT *, applying server-side filtering, and using server-side cursors or paging mechanisms reduce memory consumption and network traffic. FireDAC's capability to define rowset properties, such as FetchOptions.Mode = fmOnDemand, allows fetching data incrementally, improving perceived performance in user interfaces.

Delphi also allows embedding complex SQL statements involving joins, subqueries, window functions, and stored procedures directly into query components, preserving transactional integrity and leveraging database processing power. However, crafting such queries demands attention to execution plans and query cost. Profiling query execution with database-provided tools (e.g., SQL Server Profiler, EXPLAIN PLAN in Oracle/PostgreSQL) is invaluable to detect bottlenecks and guide adjustments such as adding hints or restructuring joins.

Effective query refactoring involves decomposing complex queries into intermediate steps or views to simplify execution and reuse. When a query performs poorly due to repeated expensive calculations, materialized views or indexed views can be employed for precomputed results.

Key optimization strategies include:

- Use parameterized queries to safeguard and optimize execution plans.

- Ensure predicates align with indexed columns to facilitate index seeks.

- Avoid functions on indexed columns within WHERE clauses.

- Explicitly define transaction boundaries to maintain data integrity.

- Minimize selected columns and rows through precise filtering.

- Utilize server-side pagination and on-demand fetching for large datasets.

- Profile queries with database tools and refine based on execution plans.

- Leverage stored procedures and views to centralize and optimize logic.

Understanding the interplay between Delphi's data access components and the underlying database system's operation is paramount. This includes recognizing how command batching, prepared statements, connection pooling, and caching mechanisms influence overall throughput. FireDAC's robust support for these features, when properly configured, aids in achieving an optimal balance between responsiveness, concurrency, and consistency.

In environments subject to heavy load or high-frequency transactions, additional considerations involve optimizing connection management to minimize overhead and prevent bottlenecks. Employing connection pools, limiting transaction scope duration, and carefully choosing isolation levels tailored to the workload are essential pragmatic measures.

The combination of secure, parameterized SQL integration tightly coupled with methodical query optimization and transaction strategy elevates Delphi applications to efficiently and safely handle complex data scenarios. This foundation is critical for building scalable, maintainable systems where data integrity and performance are non-negotiable requirements.

4.6. Data Validation and Integrity Enforcement

Robust system design necessitates the enforcement of rigorous data validation and integrity constraints to sustain correctness, reliability, and trustworthiness of applications throughout their lifecycle. This enforcement spans multiple layers, integrating business rules, domain-specific constraints, and systematic validation mechanisms, forming a coherent architecture that rejects erroneous or malformed data as early as possible.

At the core of data integrity enforcement lies the distinction between *syntactic validation* and *semantic validation*. Syntactic validation ensures that data satisfies fundamental format and type requirements, such as string length, numeric ranges, and type conformance. Semantic validation verifies that the data respects domain-specific rules and business logic, often involving cross-field consistency and contextual correctness. Balancing these strategies is vital for reducing system failures and avoiding propagation of corrupt data.

Business Rule Implementation

Business rules encode organizational policies and operational procedures that govern permissible data states and transitions. These rules manifest as constraints on attributes, relationships, or state machines within the application's domain model. Business rule enforcement can be implemented at various integration points:

- **User interface layer**: provides immediate feedback to users, limiting entry of invalid data before submission. Common techniques include regular expressions, dropdown selections, and conditional UI controls.

- **Application logic layer**: hosts comprehensive validation routines responding to complex rules that require contextual awareness, such as cross-field dependencies, time validity, and user role authorizations.

- **Persistence layer**: database constraints (e.g., CHECK, UNIQUE, FOREIGN KEY) deliver final product guarantees, preventing invalid states even in cases of application layer oversights or concurrent modifications.

Centralizing business rule definitions minimizes inconsistency and eases maintenance. Declarative specification languages or domain-specific languages (DSLs) that articulate rules independently of imperative code bases promote reusability and traceability. For example, a rule stating "Order quantity must not exceed available inventory" can be formally modeled and enforced systematically wherever relevant.

Domain Constraint Management

Domain constraints define allowable value ranges, reference integrity, and state rules grounded in real-world semantics. Effective management of these constraints integrates static and dynamic checking methods:

- **Static domain constraints** are typically enforced through type systems, schema definitions, and configuration files. For instance, enforcing an IPv4 address format, a date range within business hours, or permitted enumeration values can use static validators embedded within parsers or serialization frameworks.

- **Dynamic domain constraints** involve runtime checks that depend on temporal, environmental, or contextual parameters. For example, validating that a promotional discount applies only to active campaigns, or that a loan approval respects dynamic credit limits computed from external data sources.

Maintaining consistency across distributed components requires replicable and portable domain definitions. Approaches such as schema evolution support enable systems to adapt constraints dynamically without violating existing data integrity assumptions. Validation rules sculpted as composable functions facilitate modularity and testing, crucial for evolving business domains.

Maintaining Data Correctness Throughout the Application Lifecycle

Data correctness must extend beyond initial validation to encompass continuous integrity checks as data flows through transformation, storage, and retrieval stages. Lifelong correctness mechanisms include:

- **Input sanitization**: Prevents injection attacks and malformed inputs by escaping or rejecting suspicious characters or structures immediately on entry.

- **Transactional integrity**: Leveraging atomic transactions and rollback mechanisms preserves consistency amid concurrent operations and failures. Isolation levels and locking strategies mitigate race conditions and dirty reads.

- **Audit trails and validation hooks**: Persisting metadata about data modifications enables anomaly detection, forensics, and rollback to known-good states. Hooks triggered on create, update, or delete events ensure business logic remains enforced even with external data injections.

- **Automated tests and validation suites**: Periodic validation jobs, unit tests, and integration tests verify that data remains valid against shifting rules or migrations. Constraints embedded in test cases act as contract checks between evolving components.

A practical example can illustrate these principles. Consider a financial application handling credit card transactions subject to strict compliance rules. At the user interface, client-side validation enforces format and length constraints on card numbers. In the application backend, business rules verify that transaction amounts align with predefined credit limits, and expiration dates are valid per the current date. The database schema incorporates foreign key constraints linking cards to authorized users and CHECK constraints ensuring non-negative balances. Transactional controls maintain atomicity during multi-step payment processing to prevent double charges or inconsistencies. Finally, audit logs capture each transaction state change for downstream compliance audits.

Programmatic Enforcement Strategies

Implementing validation logic in code requires clear, maintainable constructs. Object-oriented and functional paradigms offer patterns for encapsulating validation:

```
public class Order {
    private int quantity;
    private int availableInventory;

    public Order(int quantity, int availableInventory) {
        if(quantity <= 0) {
            throw new IllegalArgumentException("Quantity must be
        positive");
        }
        if(quantity > availableInventory) {
            throw new IllegalStateException("Quantity exceeds
        inventory");
        }
        this.quantity = quantity;
        this.availableInventory = availableInventory;
    }

    // Additional methods...
}
```

In this example, constructor guards enforce critical business rules preventing the creation of orders with invalid quantities. Similar assertions may exist deeper in the call stack or within validation frameworks, ensuring invariant preservation.

Summary of Best Practices

- Validate data as close to the source of entry as possible to reduce attack surface and propagation of invalid states.

- Employ multi-layered validation encompassing syntactic, semantic, and contextual rules.

- Define business rules declaratively and centralize them to minimize duplication.

- Use database constraints as the ultimate safeguard to prevent persistence of invalid data.

- Continuously monitor, audit, and test data validity throughout the system lifecycle.

- Design validation logic to be composable, testable, and adaptable to business evolution.

Adopting these comprehensive approaches creates resilient systems that maintain high data integrity under operational stresses, regulatory demands, and evolving business requirements, thereby significantly enhancing application reliability and user trust.

Chapter 5

Delphi for Modern Network and Web Applications

Delphi is not just a powerhouse for desktop applications; it excels at building secure, high-performance network and web solutions. This chapter illuminates how Delphi meets the demands of today's interconnected world—combining efficient protocol design, real-time communication, and robust web service integration into seamless experiences. Unlock the tools and techniques that empower your applications to thrive across networks, the web, and the cloud.

5.1. Socket Programming and Protocol Design

Socket programming serves as the fundamental mechanism to enable communication between processes over a network. In Delphi, access to low-level TCP and UDP socket operations offers the flexibility to implement custom protocols tailored to specific application requirements. Understanding the underlying socket APIs, coupled with principles of protocol engineering, is critical for creating efficient, high-throughput networked systems capable of scaling with growing connection demands.

At its core, socket programming abstracts the network communication endpoint as a socket descriptor. Delphi's TClientSocket and TServerSocket components provide higher-level abstractions, but for granular control, the Windows API or Indy library can be leveraged to manipulate sockets directly. TCP sockets, built on a reliable, connection-oriented stream, guarantee ordered delivery, making them ideal for protocols requiring strict data integrity. Conversely, UDP supports connectionless datagrams, offering low-latency transmission where occasional packet loss is tolerable.

A minimal example of creating a TCP server socket using the Winsock API in Delphi involves the following steps: initialization of the socket library, creating a socket with socket() specifying the address family, type (SOCK_STREAM for TCP), and protocol; binding the socket to an IP address and port using bind(); placing the socket in listening mode with listen(); and finally accepting incoming connections via accept() in a blocking or non-blocking manner.

```
var
  ListenSock, ClientSock: TSocket;
  Addr: TSockAddrIn;
begin
  WSAStartup($0202, WSAData);
  ListenSock := socket(AF_INET, SOCK_STREAM, IPPROTO_TCP);
  Addr.sin_family := AF_INET;
  Addr.sin_port := htons(Port);
  Addr.sin_addr.S_addr := INADDR_ANY;
  bind(ListenSock, Addr, SizeOf(Addr));
  listen(ListenSock, SOMAXCONN);
  while True do
  begin
    ClientSock := accept(ListenSock, nil, nil);
    if ClientSock <> INVALID_SOCKET then
    begin
      // Handle client connection
    end;
```

```
  end;
  WSACleanup;
end;
```

For UDP sockets, the setup involves creating a socket specifying SOCK_DGRAM for the type, and then using `sendto()` and `recvfrom()` for data transmission without the connection establishment overhead. UDP is particularly suitable when implementing custom protocols that embed their own sequencing, reliability, and flow control mechanisms.

Designing custom network protocols starts with defining message framing to delineate individual messages in a continuous stream (TCP) or datagram sequence (UDP). A common approach is a length-prefixed header, where the first few bytes indicate the payload size, enabling receivers to buffer data until full messages are accrued. Fixed-size headers are often employed for protocol versioning, command identifiers, and metadata such as flags or checksums.

Efficient handling of high-throughput scenarios demands the use of asynchronous or non-blocking sockets to avoid blocking the main thread on I/O operations. Delphi applications can implement these using overlapped I/O with Windows APIs or via event-driven frameworks like Indy's asynchronous components. Careful buffer management, including pre-allocating receive buffers and minimizing memory copies, reduces latency and CPU overhead.

Scalable server architectures typically separate connection acceptance from request processing. One common pattern is the thread-per-connection model, where newly accepted sockets are handled by dedicated worker threads. While straightforward, this approach may not scale effectively with thousands of concurrent connections due to thread context-switch and resource overhead. More scalable patterns include thread pools coupled with asynchronous I/O or utilizing non-blocking sockets integrated with event multiplexing mechanisms such as IOCP (I/O Completion

Ports) on Windows.

```
var
  FdSet: TFdSet;
  TimeVal: TTimeVal;
  Buffer: array[0..1023] of Byte;
  BytesRead: Integer;
begin
  FD_ZERO(FdSet);
  FD_SET(ClientSock, FdSet);
  TimeVal.tv_sec := 0;
  TimeVal.tv_usec := 100000; // 100 ms timeout
  if select(0, @FdSet, nil, nil, @TimeVal) > 0 then
  begin
    BytesRead := recv(ClientSock, Buffer, SizeOf(Buffer), 0);
    if BytesRead > 0 then
    begin
      // Process received data
    end;
  end;
end;
```

Protocol reliability often mandates the integration of custom acknowledgment, retransmission, and heartbeat messages at the application layer when using UDP. This design mimics TCP-like guarantees while offering the flexibility to optimize latency and throughput. Alternatively, TCP-based protocols can benefit from additional flow control and congestion avoidance mechanisms tailored to the specific usage pattern.

Mastering socket programming in Delphi at a low level equips developers with the capability to build robust, high-performance network protocols aligned with precise application demands. Leveraging appropriate socket types, designing clear message structures, employing non-blocking and asynchronous patterns, and architecting scalable services collectively achieve optimal network communication performance at both protocol and application layers.

5.2. RESTful Services and WebBroker

Delphi's WebBroker framework offers a robust and versatile platform for creating and consuming RESTful APIs, aligning well with the growing demands of modern web services and distributed applications. Constructing REST APIs with WebBroker involves building HTTP-based services that expose resources via URIs, adhering to REST principles such as statelessness, uniform interface, and resource manipulation through standard HTTP methods like GET, POST, PUT, and DELETE.

At the core of WebBroker's RESTful API development is the use of `TWebModule` components, which act as containers for `TWebActionItem` instances. Each action corresponds to a particular endpoint or resource operation. By properly configuring URL mappings and HTTP method filters, these modules allow fine-grained routing control to deliver RESTful behaviors.

The essential REST action handling pattern involves examining the request's method and parameters, processing the service logic accordingly, and returning JSON or XML formatted responses with appropriate HTTP status codes. Leveraging Delphi's native JSON classes, such as `TJSONObject` and `TJSONArray`, facilitates seamless serialization and deserialization of data payloads. Integration with third-party libraries can be applied for more complex JSON schema validations or transformations.

Secure authentication in RESTful WebBroker services can be implemented effectively through token-based schemes, most commonly OAuth 2.0 or JSON Web Tokens (JWT). WebBroker's request lifecycle allows insertion of authentication handlers within the `OnBeforeDispatch` event of the `TWebModule`. These handlers inspect incoming requests for the presence and validity of access tokens. Token verification generally involves cryptographic validation of JWT signatures or introspection endpoints for OAuth tokens, followed by establishing an authenticated user context.

Combining HTTPS transport with well-implemented API key restrictions and rate-limiting techniques fortifies REST services against common vulnerabilities such as replay attacks or brute-force attempts. The use of secure cookie flags and HTTP headers (e.g., `Authorization`, `WWW-Authenticate`) according to RFC 6750 ensures interoperability with client frameworks.

API versioning is pivotal to maintaining backward compatibility while evolving the service interface. WebBroker supports URI path versioning strategies by structuring endpoints hierarchically-for example, `/api/v1/resource` and `/api/v2/resource`. Alternatively, versioning via HTTP headers, such as a custom `Accept` header specifying a media type version, can be supported by inspecting and branching logic in the request handler.

A practical approach to versioning in WebBroker is to create separate `TWebModule` instances or distinct `TWebActionItems` for each API version, isolating changes and simplifying maintenance. This segregation enables gradual deprecation of older versions and seamless client migration. Additionally, version negotiation logic can be centralized in middleware-style event handlers to direct requests dynamically.

Integration with modern web ecosystems requires supporting CORS (Cross-Origin Resource Sharing) to permit browser-based applications-single-page applications (SPAs) or progressive web apps (PWAs)-to consume REST services across domains. WebBroker modules can inject appropriate CORS headers (`Access-Control-Allow-Origin`, `Access-Control-Allow-Methods`, `Access-Control-Allow-Headers`) during preflight and actual requests, often implemented in the `OnBeforeDispatch` event handler.

Furthermore, WebBroker REST APIs can be enhanced with hypermedia controls, such as HATEOAS (Hypermedia As The Engine Of Application State), by embedding links within JSON responses. These links guide clients through available state transitions, improving discoverability and interaction flexibility. Although Delphi does not provide direct HATEOAS utilities, developers can manually construct link relations in JSON objects consistent with

RESTful API patterns.

The seamless consumption of RESTful services created with Web-Broker is supported by Delphi's THTTPClient and the REST.Client framework. These clients enable sophisticated HTTP method invocations, header management, request payload encoding, and response parsing. By abstracting HTTP intricacies, they expedite the development of Delphi-based consumers for internal or third-party APIs.

Consider the following illustrative example demonstrating a simple WebBroker REST endpoint handling GET and POST requests with JSON data exchange:

```
procedure TWebModule1.WebModule1ActionHandlerAction(Sender:
    TObject;
  Request: TWebRequest; Response: TWebResponse; var Handled:
    Boolean);
var
  LJSONRequest , LJSONResponse: TJSONObject;
begin
  Response.ContentType := 'application/json';
  if Request.Method = 'GET' then
  begin
    LJSONResponse := TJSONObject.Create;
    try
      LJSONResponse.AddPair('message', 'Welcome to REST API');
      Response.Content := LJSONResponse.ToJSON;
    finally
      LJSONResponse.Free;
    end;
  end
  else if Request.Method = 'POST' then
  begin
    LJSONRequest := TJSONObject.ParseJSONValue(Request.Content)
     as TJSONObject;
    try
      // Process the request data
      if Assigned(LJSONRequest) and (LJSONRequest.GetValue('input
      ') <> nil) then
      begin
        LJSONResponse := TJSONObject.Create;
        try
          LJSONResponse.AddPair('output', LJSONRequest.GetValue('
        input').Value.ToUpper);
          Response.Content := LJSONResponse.ToJSON;
        finally
          LJSONResponse.Free;
```

```
        end;
    end
    else
    begin
      Response.StatusCode := 400;
      Response.Content := '{"error":"Invalid JSON payload"}';
    end;
  finally
    LJSONRequest.Free;
  end;
  end
  else
  begin
    Response.StatusCode := 405; // Method Not Allowed
    Response.Content := '{"error":"Method not supported"}';
  end;
  Handled := True;
end;
```

The example highlights key REST concepts: method-based branching, JSON serialization, and response construction with correct content types and HTTP status codes.

WebBroker enables Delphi developers to design RESTful services that support secure authentication, API versioning, and seamless integration with client-side ecosystems. Leveraging event-driven request handling, JSON processing capabilities, and HTTP protocol features, architectures built on WebBroker form reliable backbones for modern web and mobile applications, complementing Delphi's strengths with RESTful design principles.

5.3. SOAP and Legacy Web Service Integration

Delphi's comprehensive support for SOAP (Simple Object Access Protocol) web services facilitates robust integration with legacy enterprise systems, which often rely on this protocol for interoperability. SOAP, a protocol designed to enable communication across heterogeneous environments, leverages XML for message format and typically operates over HTTP or HTTPS transport layers. Effective integration with legacy SOAP services requires careful attention to service contract adherence, message serialization formats, security constraints, and performance considerations within the Delphi runtime environment.

Delphi provides a dedicated SOAP client and server framework, enabling seamless binding to WSDL (Web Services Description Language) documents. The integrated WSDL importer automates the generation of interface declarations and serialization code, encapsulating complex XML data types and service operations into native Delphi class structures. This abstraction permits developers to invoke legacy SOAP operations as strongly typed methods, significantly reducing manual XML manipulation and encoding errors.

The generated interfaces typically descend from IInvokable, the core abstraction for Delphi's remote method invocation. Implementing or consuming these interfaces enforces strict adherence to the WSDL's method signatures, ensuring contract compatibility. Delphi's runtime marshals method parameters to compliant SOAP envelopes and handles response deserialization, transparently managing XML schema data types such as xsd:string, xsd:int, and complex structures.

Legacy SOAP services often impose strict adherence to WS-I (Web Services Interoperability) Basic Profile standards and legacy SOAP versions (1.1 or 1.2). Delphi's SOAP runtime supports customization of SOAP headers, namespaces, and encoding styles (literal vs. encoded), which are critical adjustments when interfacing with non-conforming legacy services. Developers must explicitly confirm whether the service uses RPC or document style messaging, as this affects the generated WSDL and binding strategies.

Custom serialization handlers may be necessary for unusual or extended XML schemas, where automatic code generation does not capture all nuances such as choice elements, substitution groups, or polymorphic hierarchies. Extending serialization classes involves overriding methods of TRemotable descendants, allowing precise control over XML node generation. This is essential when integrating with legacy services that expect strict SOAP body formatting.

Security in legacy SOAP services often centers on WS-Security standards, which introduce mechanisms for message integrity and confidentiality through XML Signature and XML Encryption. Delphi's native SOAP library does not directly support WS-Security extensions; therefore, security must be enforced at transport or application layers. The predominant best practice is to secure SOAP communication using HTTPS, which ensures channel-level encryption and server authentication.

For environments requiring message-level security, custom implementations are necessary. This typically involves intercepting SOAP envelopes pre-transmission and post-reception to insert or validate security tokens, timestamps, and signatures. Developers may employ the THTTPReqResp component to gain access to raw HTTP requests and responses, enabling the injection of WS-Security headers via DOM manipulation of the SOAP envelopes.

Credential management often involves using Basic HTTP Authentication or client certificates configured in the underlying THTTPRIO component. Enterprise reliability mandates the frequent rotation of credentials and secure storage mechanisms, such as encrypting configuration files or integrating with secure vaults.

Legacy SOAP web services can exhibit significant latency and throughput constraints due to verbose XML payloads and synchronous communication patterns. Delphi applications must mitigate these issues through multiple architectural and coding best practices.

- **Connection Reuse:** Configuring the THTTPRIO component to maintain persistent connections via HTTP keep-alive reduces socket overhead and accelerates sequential requests.

- **Asynchronous Invocation:** Employing multi-threaded

designs or Delphi's asynchronous patterns to prevent UI blocking fosters responsiveness in client applications during network-bound operations.

- **Message Compression:** Although SOAP itself does not mandate compression, intervening proxies or custom server-side support for HTTP gzip encoding can reduce bandwidth consumption. Delphi's HTTP client components can support this via header customization.

- **Selective Field Requests:** When supported by the legacy service, limiting data retrieval to essential fields minimizes XML envelope size and parsing costs.

- **Caching Strategies:** Implementing client-side response caching for idempotent operations reduces repetitive network calls. This is especially effective for frequently requested static data.

Profiling and diagnostic tools such as Wireshark or Fiddler facilitate the examination of SOAP message exchanges to identify bottlenecks, schema mismatches, or security failures. Delphi's ability to hook into SOAP message lifecycle events also supports granular logging, enabling reproducibility of interoperability issues.

A concise example demonstrates Delphi's consumption of a legacy SOAP endpoint. Assuming a WSDL at `http://legacyserver/service?wsdl`, the WSDL importer generates an interface `ILegacyService` exposing method `GetCustomerData` which returns a complex type `TCustomer`.

```
var
  Service: ILegacyService;
  Customer: TCustomer;
begin
  Service := GetILegacyService(True, 'http://legacyserver/service
    ');
  try
    Customer := Service.GetCustomerData('12345');
    WriteLn('Customer Name: ', Customer.Name);
    WriteLn('Account Balance: ', FloatToStr(Customer.Balance));
```

```
except
  on E: Exception do
    WriteLn('Error invoking legacy service: ', E.Message);
  end;
end;
```

The call to GetCustomerData performs XML serialization of the input parameter, sends the SOAP request, and deserializes the structured response into the TCustomer Delphi object. Error handling captures communication or serialization failures, which are common when interfacing with legacy endpoints.

- Always derive client stubs using Delphi's WSDL importer to maintain strict WSDL contract fidelity.

- Verify SOAP versions, encoding styles, and message formats against legacy service documentation.

- Use HTTPS transport to secure authentication credentials and message confidentiality.

- Introduce custom serialization for non-standard XML constructs and WS-Security message layer requirements.

- Profile and optimize network usage with connection reuse, asynchronous processing, and payload minimization.

- Employ rigorous error reporting and logging to diagnose interoperability issues in heterogeneous enterprise contexts.

Effectively integrating legacy SOAP web services in Delphi requires marrying automated framework capabilities with bespoke adjustments for schema conformance, security enhancements, and performance tuning. Such rigor enables the continued viability and modernization of legacy applications within contemporary enterprise architectures.

5.4. JSON, XML, and Data Serialization

Delphi offers robust support for structured data interchange formats, notably JSON and XML, which are fundamental in modern integration scenarios. This section delves into advanced methodologies for parsing, validating, and serializing these formats, emphasizing performance and reliability inherent to Delphi's libraries.

Delphi's System.JSON unit provides classes such as TJSONObject, TJSONArray, and TJSONValue that enable fine-grained manipulation of JSON data. Beyond basic parsing, Delphi supports streaming JSON data using TJsonTextReader and TJsonTextWriter, allowing efficient handling of large datasets without loading entire structures into memory.

Parsing complex JSON structures often involves recursive traversal coupled with type assertions. Consider the pattern for robust parsing with validation to ensure conformity with expected schema elements:

```
function ParsePersonJSON(const JSONStr: string): TPerson;
var
  JSONObject: TJSONObject;
  NameValue, AgeValue: TJSONValue;
begin
  JSONObject := TJSONObject.ParseJSONValue(JSONStr) as
    TJSONObject;
  try
    if not Assigned(JSONObject) then
      raise Exception.Create('Invalid JSON format');

    NameValue := JSONObject.GetValue('name');
    AgeValue := JSONObject.GetValue('age');

    if (NameValue = nil) or (AgeValue = nil) then
      raise Exception.Create('Missing required keys');

    Result.Name := NameValue.Value;
    Result.Age := StrToIntDef(AgeValue.Value, -1);

    if Result.Age < 0 then
      raise Exception.Create('Invalid age value');
  finally
```

117

```
    JSONObject.Free;
  end;
end;
```

This code snippet highlights the importance of explicit validation steps when parsing JSON, preventing silent failures or corrupt data ingestion. For scenarios requiring JSON schema validation, third-party libraries or custom validators can be integrated, but Delphi's native classes provide foundations for enforcing correctness during deserialization.

Serialization to JSON in Delphi can be optimized by avoiding intermediate string concatenations and leveraging streaming APIs. For example:

```
procedure SerializePersonsToJSON(const Persons: TArray<TPerson>;
    Stream: TStream);
var
  Writer: TJsonTextWriter;
  StringWriter: TStringWriter;
  I: Integer;
begin
  StringWriter := TStringWriter.Create;
  try
    Writer := TJsonTextWriter.Create(StringWriter);
    try
      Writer.Formatting := TJsonFormatting.None;
      Writer.WriteStartArray;
      for I := 0 to Length(Persons) - 1 do
      begin
        Writer.WriteStartObject;
        Writer.WritePropertyName('name');
        Writer.WriteValue(Persons[I].Name);
        Writer.WritePropertyName('age');
        Writer.WriteValue(Persons[I].Age);
        Writer.WriteEndObject;
      end;
      Writer.WriteEndArray;
      Writer.Flush;

      Stream.WriteBuffer(Pointer(StringWriter.ToString)^, Length(
      StringWriter.ToString) * SizeOf(Char));
    finally
      Writer.Free;
    end;
  finally
    StringWriter.Free;
  end;
```

```
end;
```

This streaming approach ensures minimal memory overhead, allowing the serialization of large collections efficiently. Setting Formatting to None produces compact JSON output, while TJsonFormatting.Indented can be specified for human-readable results.

Delphi's Xml.XMLDoc and Xml.XMLIntf units provide comprehensive support for XML document manipulation through interfaces such as IXMLDocument and nodes via IXMLNode. Parsing XML follows a tree model, but for large files or streaming requirements, SAX-like parsers can be integrated externally.

To parse an XML document securely and validate against an XSD schema, Delphi leverages MSXML or other platform XML parsers, exposing their validation capabilities. The following outlines loading and schema validation:

```
var
  XMLDoc: IXMLDocument;
begin
  XMLDoc := TXMLDocument.Create(nil);
  XMLDoc.LoadFromFile('data.xml');
  XMLDoc.Options := XMLDoc.Options + [doValidateOnParse];
  XMLDoc.SchemaLocation := 'data.xsd';
  try
    XMLDoc.ValidateDocument;
  except
    on E: Exception do
      raise Exception.CreateFmt('XML Validation failed: %s', [E.
      Message]);
  end;
  // Processing continues assuming valid XML structure
end;
```

This method enforces strict compliance with XML schemas, crucial for enterprise-level data integration where format correctness is mandatory.

While manual construction of XML via IXMLNode interfaces is possible, Delphi supports automating this process through RTTI-driven serialization frameworks such as XmlSerializer components or custom converters. The following pattern demonstrates manual XML serialization for an object graph:

```
procedure SerializePersonToXML(const Person: TPerson; Node:
    IXMLNode);
begin
  Node.ChildNodes['Name'].NodeValue := Person.Name;
  Node.ChildNodes['Age'].NodeValue := Person.Age;
end;
```

In large-scale systems, adopting schema-driven approaches with code generation tools expedites mapping complex data types, ensuring consistency and maintainability.

Delphi's native JSON and XML parsers are optimized for speed and reliability, but several best practices enhance integration outcomes:

- Use streaming APIs when dealing with large datasets to minimize memory consumption.

- Validate data early to prevent propagation of malformed or incomplete data.

- Leverage schema validation for XML and, where applicable, for JSON to guarantee data integrity in heterogeneous environments.

- Employ compact serialization to optimize network transmission, switching to indented formatting when debugging or logging.

- Integrate with platform-specific capabilities (e.g., MSXML on Windows) to extend validation and parsing functionalities.

Delphi's support for both JSON and XML, combined with its powerful RTTI and streaming mechanisms, equips developers to create high-performance, reliable data interchange layers within modern distributed applications.

5.5. Real-time Communications and SignalR Patterns

Real-time communication demands low-latency, bidirectional data exchange capabilities, which are essential for applications such as collaborative platforms, live dashboards, and instant messaging. Achieving scalability and responsiveness in Delphi-based systems involves leveraging contemporary architectural models such as WebSockets, publish/subscribe (pub/sub) paradigms, and SignalR-like frameworks adapted to Delphi's ecosystem.

WebSockets provide the fundamental protocol enabling persistent, full-duplex communication channels over a single TCP connection. This contrasts with traditional HTTP request-response cycles by maintaining an open connection, minimizing overhead, and supporting asynchronous messages initiated by both client and server. Delphi's support for WebSockets is available through libraries like Indy and third-party components, which facilitate connection management, message framing, and event-driven handling.

Implementing WebSocket communication in Delphi requires efficient event loops and concurrency management to handle multiple simultaneous connections without blocking. The sample code below outlines a minimalist WebSocket server snippet that accepts incoming connections and echoes back received messages asynchronously:

```
procedure TWebSocketServer.OnMessage(Sender: TObject; const Msg:
    string);
begin
  // Echo the received message back to the client
  TWebSocketConnection(Sender).SendMessage(Msg);
end;

procedure TWebSocketServer.OnConnect(Sender: TObject);
begin
  // Initialize connection-specific resources here
  TWebSocketConnection(Sender).OnMessage := OnMessage;
```

```
end;

procedure TWebSocketServer.Start;
begin
  FListener := TIdTCPServer.Create(nil);
  FListener.DefaultPort := 8080;
  FListener.OnConnect := OnConnect;
  FListener.Active := True;
end;
```

Extending beyond raw WebSocket usage, the pub/sub pattern abstracts state propagation by decoupling message senders (publishers) from receivers (subscribers). This is critical for scalability since it enables system components to operate independently, improving modularity and load distribution. Within Delphi, this can be achieved by integrating message brokers such as RabbitMQ, ZeroMQ, or Redis Pub/Sub, tailored to handle domain-specific topics or channels.

A robust pub/sub system facilitates features like selective message filtering, topic-based subscriptions, and persistent event logging. Consider a collaborative editing application: when a user modifies a document segment, the change is published to a topic representing that document. All subscribed client endpoints receive the update in near real-time, ensuring consistency of shared state.

SignalR, originally designed for the .NET environment, elegantly integrates real-time capabilities with automatic fallback options between WebSockets, Server-Sent Events (SSE), and long-polling. SignalR's hub-based model offers an abstraction where clients can invoke methods on the server and vice versa, simplifying development by masking transport details. Porting SignalR-like architectures to Delphi involves replicating core concepts:

- **Hubs**: Centralized endpoints managing groups of connections and routing messages.

- **Connection Lifetime Management**: Handling reconnections and state restoration.

- **Protocols**: Using JSON or Protobuf for message serialization.

A Delphi implementation can be built atop WebSocket servers, layered with a lightweight messaging protocol. For instance, employing JSON-RPC over WebSockets permits invoking remote procedures while preserving a clear method-call semantic. The following pseudocode demonstrates how to model a hub receiving a client method invocation and broadcasting results:

```
type
  TSignalRHub = class
  private
    FConnections: TObjectList<TWebSocketConnection>;
  public
    procedure OnClientMethod(const Conn: TWebSocketConnection;
      const Method: string; const Params: TJSONValue);
    procedure Broadcast(const Method: string; const Params:
      TJSONValue);
  end;

procedure TSignalRHub.OnClientMethod(const Conn:
    TWebSocketConnection; const Method: string; const Params:
    TJSONValue);
begin
  if Method = 'SendMessage' then
    Broadcast('ReceiveMessage', Params);
end;

procedure TSignalRHub.Broadcast(const Method: string; const
    Params: TJSONValue);
var
  Msg: TJSONObject;
  Conn: TWebSocketConnection;
begin
  Msg := TJSONObject.Create;
  try
    Msg.AddPair('method', Method);
    Msg.AddPair('params', Params.Clone as TJSONValue);
    for Conn in FConnections do
      Conn.SendMessage(Msg.ToString);
  finally
    Msg.Free;
  end;
end;
```

The above pattern supports group messaging and coordination for real-time collaboration in Delphi applications. To enhance scalability, hubs can be distributed across multiple nodes, synchronized via an external state manager, or connected through message brokers.

Latency minimization techniques include batching updates, delta compression of changes, and prioritizing messages through quality-of-service queues. Additionally, for mobile or bandwidth-constrained clients, adaptive algorithms that adjust update frequencies based on network conditions can be implemented.

Security considerations are paramount. Real-time channels should use secure WebSocket protocols (`wss://`) with TLS encryption. Authentication tokens or API keys validated on connection establish secure sessions, mitigating unauthorized access to real-time streams. Access control can be further enforced by dynamically assigning connection groups or topics based on user roles.

In the context of user experience, real-time communication patterns must be integrated with user interface event loops to avoid blocking UI responsiveness. Delphi's `TThread` or `System.Threading` library can be leveraged to manage background processing of message dispatch and reception, updating visual components asynchronously via synchronization mechanisms.

Combining these principles creates a foundation for building sophisticated, scalable, and responsive Delphi applications. Examples include stock trading terminals streaming live quotes, multiplayer game servers managing player actions, and IoT dashboards processing streaming sensor data. Mastery of WebSockets, pub-/sub models, and SignalR-like architectural patterns enables developers to architect solutions that harmonize performance with maintainability in real-time communication ecosystems.

5.6. Security in Networked Applications

Security in networked applications is paramount, particularly when sensitive data traverses potentially untrusted environments. Ensuring confidentiality, integrity, and authenticity requires a layered approach involving cryptographic implementations, secure transport protocols, and meticulous certificate management. When building networked Delphi applications, these safeguards collectively protect data and user interactions from interception, tampering, and impersonation.

At the core of application security is cryptography, which provides mechanisms for encryption, decryption, and digital signatures. In Delphi, cryptographic functionality can be implemented via libraries such as the System.Hash unit for hashing and third-party libraries like OpenSSL or DCPCrypt for symmetric and asymmetric encryption algorithms.

Symmetric encryption algorithms (e.g., AES) are optimal for securing bulk data communications due to their performance efficiency. Asymmetric algorithms (e.g., RSA or Elliptic Curve Cryptography) facilitate secure key exchanges and digital signatures, ensuring authenticity and nonrepudiation. Secure random number generators (RNGs), critical for key generation and nonce creation, must comply with cryptographic standards to prevent predictability.

Transport Layer Security (TLS) is the industry standard for securing communications over networks. TLS operates above the transport layer, providing encrypted channels that protect data in transit from eavesdropping and man-in-the-middle attacks. Delphi's TIdSSLIOHandlerSocketOpenSSL component, part of Indy components, enables integration of OpenSSL-based TLS functionality into client and server applications.

To enforce best practices in TLS usage, applications should:

- Utilize the latest stable TLS versions (TLS 1.2 or 1.3) and disable deprecated protocols such as SSLv3 and TLS 1.0.

- Prefer strong cipher suites, including AES-GCM or ChaCha20-Poly1305, and avoid weak or vulnerable algorithms.

- Validate server and client certificates rigorously to prevent impersonation.

- Enforce perfect forward secrecy (PFS) by preferring ephemeral key exchange algorithms like ECDHE.

An example of assigning an SSL IOHandler to an Indy HTTP client for a secure TLS connection is:

```
uses
  IdHTTP, IdSSLOpenSSL;

var
  HTTP: TIdHTTP;
  SSLHandler: TIdSSLIOHandlerSocketOpenSSL;
begin
  HTTP := TIdHTTP.Create(nil);
  SSLHandler := TIdSSLIOHandlerSocketOpenSSL.Create(HTTP);
  try
    SSLHandler.SSLOptions.Method := sslvTLSv1_2;
    SSLHandler.SSLOptions.Mode := sslmClient;
    HTTP.IOHandler := SSLHandler;

    // Perform secure HTTP request
    Memo1.Lines.Text := HTTP.Get('https://secure.example.com/api/
     data');
  finally
    SSLHandler.Free;
    HTTP.Free;
  end;
end;
```

Digital certificates underlie the trust model in TLS and secure communications. Certificates issued by trusted Certificate Authorities (CAs) authenticate endpoints by binding public keys to entity identities. Applications must properly manage certificate verification and validation workflows to prevent security gaps.

Key certificate management best practices include:

- Implement robust certificate validation, including chain-of-trust verification, expiration date checks, and revocation status assessment (via CRL or OCSP).

- Avoid blind acceptance or self-signed certificates unless explicitly trusted by the application context.

- Support certificate pinning when possible to limit trust to specific certificates or public keys, substantially mitigating man-in-the-middle risks.

- Facilitate secure storage and access to certificates and private keys, ideally leveraging platform security features such as Windows Certificate Store or encrypted storage.

Delphi's Indy SSL components enable custom certificate validation by handling the OnVerifyPeer event, where developers can implement logic to examine certificates manually or override default verification behavior.

```
procedure TForm1.IdSSLIOHandlerSocketOpenSSL1VerifyPeer(
    Certificate: TIdX509;
  AOk: Boolean; var AIgnore: Boolean);
begin
  // Example: Reject certificates with known revoked serials
  if Certificate.SerialNumber = '123456789ABCDEF' then
  begin
    AIgnore := True;  // Reject this certificate
  end
  else
  begin
    AIgnore := not AOk; // Proceed only if default validation
      passed
  end;
end;
```

Authentication mechanisms establish the identity of users or systems before granting resource access. Common strategies include username/password logins, token-based authentication (e.g., OAuth or JWT), and certificate-based client authentication in TLS.

Session security complements authentication by preserving the authenticated context securely over time. Strategies to enforce session security include:

- Using short-lived session tokens protected by secure transport layers.

- Employing cryptographically strong session identifiers resistant to prediction or fixation.

- Implementing replay attack mitigations such as nonce usage or timestamp validation.

- Encrypting any client-stored session state, such as cookies or local data.

- Keeping session timeouts and re-authentication thresholds to limit exposure.

In Delphi applications leveraging RESTful APIs, tokens can be managed in the HTTP headers to maintain authenticated sessions:

```
HTTP.Request.CustomHeaders.Values['Authorization'] := 'Bearer ' +
    AccessToken;
ResponseContent := HTTP.Get('https://secure.example.com/user/
    profile');
```

Data protection extends beyond encryption in transport. Sensitive data must be securely handled at all stages: input, in-memory processing, storage, and output. Techniques include:

- Minimizing sensitive data exposure by applying the principle of least privilege.

- Zeroing buffers or memory after use to avoid residual data in RAM.

- Encrypting sensitive configuration parameters or database records using strong encryption keys isolated from application code.

- Avoiding logging of sensitive information such as passwords, keys, or personally identifiable information (PII).

Delphi's secure memory handling can be augmented with specialized libraries that provide zeroization and guarded memory allocations to minimize risk of data leakage.

- Always use up-to-date, well-vetted cryptographic libraries and protocols.

- Rigorously validate and manage certificates; implement pinning where feasible.

- Enforce secure authentication and session management aligned with threat models.

- Protect sensitive data holistically from input to storage and transmission.

- Regularly update your application dependencies to incorporate security patches.

Following these principles in Delphi networked applications establishes a resilient security posture, critical for reliable operation in open and diverse network environments.

Chapter 6

Concurrency, Parallelism, and Asynchronous Programming

Harness the full computational power of modern hardware by mastering Delphi's advanced concurrency and parallelism features. This chapter explores the tools, design patterns, and debugging strategies essential for writing efficient, safe, and scalable multi-threaded applications. Whether you are unlocking parallel CPUs or architecting non-blocking user experiences, these techniques elevate your Delphi code to the next level.

6.1. Multithreading and Synchronization

Delphi provides robust support for multithreading, enabling concurrent execution within applications to improve responsiveness and performance. Threads in Delphi are primarily managed through the TThread class, forming the foundation for thread creation and control. Effective multithreading requires synchronization mechanisms to coordinate access to shared resources, prevent race conditions, and ensure data integrity. This section explores thread creation, management, and synchronization primitives including mutexes, critical sections, and semaphores, emphasizing techniques to safely access shared state.

Thread creation in Delphi typically involves extending the TThread class by overriding its Execute method, which encapsulates code run in the separate thread context. The constructor usually initializes the thread and may begin execution immediately depending on the CreateSuspended parameter passed to the inherited constructor:

```
type
  TWorkerThread = class(TThread)
  protected
    procedure Execute; override;
  public
    constructor Create(CreateSuspended: Boolean);
  end;

constructor TWorkerThread.Create(CreateSuspended: Boolean);
begin
  inherited Create(CreateSuspended);
  FreeOnTerminate := True; // Automatic cleanup on thread finish
end;

procedure TWorkerThread.Execute;
begin
  while not Terminated do
  begin
    // Thread work here
    Sleep(100); // Simulate workload
  end;
end;
```

The Terminated property facilitates cooperative thread termination by signaling the thread routine to cease execution gracefully. To start the thread, call the Start method or create it with CreateSuspended = False.

When multiple threads access shared variables or resources, unsynchronized operations risk data corruption, commonly known as race conditions. To prevent such issues, synchronization primitives are employed to serialize access, ensuring only one thread modifies the shared state at a time.

Critical Sections

Critical sections are lightweight synchronization objects that protect small sections of code from concurrent access by multiple threads within the same process. Delphi provides TCriticalSection from the SyncObjs unit:

```
var
  CS: TCriticalSection;
  SharedCounter: Integer = 0;

procedure SafeIncrement;
begin
  CS.Enter;
  try
    Inc(SharedCounter);
  finally
    CS.Leave;
  end;
end;

initialization
  CS := TCriticalSection.Create;

finalization
  CS.Free;
```

Using Enter and Leave, only one thread can execute the code modifying SharedCounter at a time. This serialization prevents inconsistent state visible from concurrent increments. Critical sections are efficient and suited for short, frequent access patterns within a process, but cannot synchronize threads across processes.

Mutexes

Mutexes extend synchronization by enabling inter-process mutual exclusion. The Delphi TMutex class wraps system mutex objects. Unlike critical sections, mutexes can block threads across different processes, making them suitable for cross-application resource protection. Mutexes are slower to acquire than critical sections due to operating system kernel involvement.

Example usage of a named mutex:

```
var
  Mutex: TMutex;

procedure AccessSharedResource;
begin
  if Mutex.WaitFor(INFINITE) = wrSignaled then
  try
    // Access resource safely
  finally
    Mutex.ReleaseMutex;
  end;
end;

initialization
  Mutex := TMutex.Create(nil, False, 'Global\\MySharedMutex');

finalization
  Mutex.Free;
```

Using a named mutex with the Global namespace allows synchronization across user sessions in Windows. Always ensure proper release of the mutex to avoid deadlocks.

Semaphores

Semaphores generalize locking primitives by allowing a fixed number of simultaneous holders, useful for controlling resource pools or throttling concurrency. The TSemaphore class in Delphi provides this functionality. A semaphore is initialized with a maximum and an initial count.

Example use limiting concurrent access to three threads:

```
var
  Semaphore: TSemaphore;

procedure UseResource;
begin
  if Semaphore.WaitFor(INFINITE) = wrSignaled then
  try
    // Protected resource usage
```

```
  finally
    Semaphore.Release;
  end;
end;

initialization
  Semaphore := TSemaphore.Create(nil, 3, 3, '');

finalization
  Semaphore.Free;
```

This pattern enables up to three threads to concurrently enter the critical region, blocking further requests until at least one thread releases the semaphore.

Safe Access to Shared State

To safely share state among threads, follow these best practices:

- **Minimize Critical Sections:** Keep the locked code minimal to reduce contention and improve performance.

- **Use Local Copies:** Operate on thread-local copies where possible, copying results back inside protected sections.

- **Avoid Nested Locks:** Nested locking risks deadlocks; order locks consistently or reconsider design.

- **Employ Atomic Operations:** For simple counters or flags, use atomic primitives like InterlockedIncrement to avoid heavy locks.

Example of using atomic operations to increment a shared counter safely without explicit locks:

```
uses
  Windows;

var
  AtomicCounter: Integer = 0;

procedure IncrementAtomic;
begin
  InterlockedIncrement(AtomicCounter);
end;
```

Atomics are faster than mutexes or critical sections but are limited to simple data types and operations.

Primitive	Use Case	Scope / Performance
Critical Section	Synchronize threads within one process	Fastest, lightweight kernel transition
Mutex	Synchronize threads across processes	Slower, can span process boundaries
Semaphore	Limit concurrency to fixed count	Useful for resource pools or throttling
Atomic Operations	Simple shared counters or flags	Very fast, limited functionality

Correct use of these primitives combined with well-designed thread control promotes safe, efficient multithreaded Delphi applications. Synchronization prevents race conditions and deadlocks, preserving system stability and data accuracy. Understanding the trade-offs between synchronization mechanisms and applying them judiciously in shared state scenarios is vital for advanced Delphi developers.

6.2. Task-based Parallelism

Delphi's task-based parallelism infrastructure centers around the TTask framework, designed to simplify the creation and management of asynchronous and concurrent computations. Unlike traditional thread management, which requires explicit handling of threads and synchronization, TTask abstracts the concurrency model into discrete, independent units of work called tasks. Each task encapsulates a callable, typically an anonymous method, which the runtime schedules for execution on the system's thread pool.

The core API for task creation involves the TTask.Create and TTask.Run methods. TTask.Create constructs a task without starting it immediately, whereas TTask.Run both creates and schedules the task for execution. This distinction provides fine-grained control over task lifecycle for scenarios requiring deferred start. Once

136

created, a task can be synchronously waited upon or checked for completion, enabling coordination between tasks or with the main thread.

```
uses
  System.Threading, System.SysUtils;

var
  Task: ITask;
begin
  Task := TTask.Create(
    procedure
    begin
      // Perform some CPU-intensive operation here
      Sleep(1000);  // Simulate work
      Writeln('Task completed.');
    end);
  Task.Start;

  // Main thread waits for the task to complete
  Task.Wait;
  Writeln('Main thread resumed.');
end;
```

Futures extend the TTask abstraction by coupling asynchronous execution with a mechanism for returning values or results from background computations. Delphi's parallel programming library supports futures via TTask.Future<TResult>, enabling tasks that compute and yield results accessible through the Value property. The future interface supports the idiomatic asynchronous programming model, where the main thread can continue processing and only access the result upon necessity, promoting responsiveness without blocking.

```
var
  Future: IFuture<Integer>;
  ResultValue: Integer;
begin
  Future := TTask.Future<Integer>(
    function: Integer
    begin
      // Heavy calculation
      Sleep(500);
      Result := 42;
    end);

  // ... other work
```

```
  ResultValue := Future.Value; // Blocks here if not finished
  Writeln('Result from future: ', ResultValue);
end;
```

Parallel loops provide a high-level pattern to divide iterations of a loop across multiple cores automatically. Delphi's TParallel class exposes a set of static methods to parallelize for loops efficiently. The method TParallel.For distributes loop iterations to different worker threads, balancing workload to maximize CPU utilization. Its usage resembles a conventional for loop but with the runtime handling the partitioning, scheduling, and synchronization.

```
var
  I: Integer;
begin
  TParallel.For(0, 999,
    procedure(Index: Integer)
    begin
      Writeln('Processing iteration ', Index);
      // Perform compute-intensive processing here
    end);
end;
```

Proper parallel workload decomposition is crucial to achieving optimal efficiency. The goal is to minimize overhead, avoid false sharing, and ensure balanced execution. Parallelism granularity must be chosen carefully: too fine-grained tasks increase scheduling overhead, while tasks too coarse can cause load imbalance and underutilize cores. Adaptive chunk sizes or workload partitioning algorithms—such as work-stealing or guided partitioning—can dynamically redistribute iterations or subtasks to maintain balance.

- TParallel.For by default applies a partitioning strategy tuned for general use cases.

- Programmers can influence this behavior through overloads that accept partitioners, enabling customized division of labor suited to specific application domains, such as processing irregular data structures or handling heterogeneous workloads.

- The primary challenge in parallel programming is simplifying code while ensuring correctness and performance.

- Delphi's task-based constructs encourage writing parallel code as declarative blocks rather than explicit thread manipulations, which reduces complexity and boilerplate.

- The use of lambda expressions and closures enables embedding synchronization context and shared state management within a local scope, easing parallel algorithm expression.

- Task cancellation and exception handling are integral to robust parallel applications. The TTask framework integrates cancellation tokens and structured exception propagation, allowing coordinated task termination and error recovery.

This alleviates the common pitfalls of unmanaged thread interruptions and unobserved exceptions.

Overall, Delphi's task-based parallelism ecosystem, combining TTask, futures, and TParallel, advances a composable, scalable approach to parallel programming. By decomposing problems into discrete, manageable tasks and leveraging efficient runtime scheduling, developers can concentrate on algorithmic logic while benefiting from modern multicore architectures. Effective use hinges on choosing appropriate granularity, balancing workloads, and adopting idiomatic constructs that reliably express parallelism with clarity and precision.

6.3. Message Queues and Asynchronous Patterns

Modern software systems frequently require non-blocking designs that maintain responsiveness under varying workload conditions. A fundamental approach to achieving this is through message-driven architectures, where communication between components occurs via message passing rather than shared state or synchronous calls. Message queues and asynchronous patterns are central to designing such systems, enabling decoupling of producers and consumers and facilitating scalable background processing.

A message queue functions as a buffer that holds messages sent from producers until they can be processed by one or more consumers. This arrangement inherently decouples the timing between message generation and processing, which allows the system to absorb sudden surges in workload and avoid blocking on synchronous operations. Essential characteristics include first-in-first-out (FIFO) ordering, persistence, and delivery guarantees that may vary from at-most-once to exactly-once semantics.

Designing effective message queues requires attention to:

- **Durability and Persistence**: To handle system failures without loss of data, queues often persist messages on stable storage before acknowledging receipt.

- **Ordering Guarantees**: Some applications require strict ordering, which may impose constraints on concurrency and partitioning.

- **Delivery Semantics**: Depending on the use case, systems may tolerate message loss (at-most-once), require guaranteed delivery (at-least-once), or prohibit duplicates (exactly-once), each with trade-offs in complexity and resource usage.

- **Load Balancing and Scalability**: Queues can be partitioned or replicated to increase throughput and availability, with mechanisms to distribute messages evenly or according to priority.

Common implementations such as RabbitMQ, Apache Kafka, and AWS SQS provide infrastructure-level support for these features, allowing developers to focus on application logic.

Asynchronous programming revolves around non-blocking operations where tasks initiate work and proceed without waiting for direct completion, relying on callbacks, promises, futures, or event loops to handle results once available. This approach prevents any single operation from holding up the main execution thread, crucial for responsive user interfaces and highly concurrent systems.

Key asynchronous models include:

- **Event-Driven Architectures**: Execution flow is driven by external or internal events, invoking handlers in reaction to message arrivals or state changes.

- **Reactive Programming**: A declarative style where data streams propagate changes automatically, often implemented via observable sequences.

- **Future/Promise Constructs**: Represent eventual completion of asynchronous operations, enabling chaining and synchronization.

Integration of asynchronous programming with message queues can enable systems where producers enqueue tasks and consumers operate independently, processing messages as resources become available.

The actor model provides a formalized pattern for managing concurrency through actors-independent entities that encapsulate state and behavior, communicate strictly via asynchronous message passing, and process messages sequentially in their own context. Actors never share mutable state directly, which sidesteps traditional concurrency hazards such as race conditions and deadlocks.

An actor's operational semantics can be summarized as:

1. **Receive** the next message from its mailbox.

2. **Process** the message atomically, updating local state and possibly spawning new actors or sending messages.

3. **Repeat** for subsequent messages.

This design lends itself particularly well to distributed systems where actors may be located across networked nodes. The actor model enables:

- **Isolation and Fault Tolerance**: Localizing state and failures simplifies recovery strategies.

- **Scalability**: Actors may be moved or replicated transparently to scale horizontally.

- **Predictable Concurrency**: Sequential message processing within actors avoids internal data races.

Frameworks such as Akka (for the JVM) and Orleans (for .NET) implement the actor model with built-in tools for messaging, supervision, and cluster management.

Several architectural patterns emerge naturally from asynchronous, message-based paradigms:

- **Command or Task Queues**: Decouple request submission from execution, optimizing workload distribution and prioritization.

- **Publish-Subscribe (Pub/Sub)**: Enable event broadcasting where multiple consumers react to published messages without tight coupling to producers.

- **Work Pools**: Distribute messages among worker actors or processes to parallelize processing, often with dynamic scaling.

- **Event Sourcing and CQRS**: Separate command handling and query activities, using append-only event stores to maintain consistent application state asynchronously.

Each pattern leverages asynchronous behavior and queues to achieve responsiveness, fault tolerance, and elasticity. For example, a user interface thread may enqueue commands rapidly without waiting for completion, while background workers consume these commands to update databases or trigger external calls. This avoids user interface freezes and improves throughput.

Illustrating asynchronous task processing, consider a simplified pseudocode example where tasks are submitted to a queue and processed by worker actors. The example uses an actor-style message loop to highlight key concepts:

```
import asyncio
from asyncio import Queue

class Worker:
    def __init__(self, task_queue):
        self.task_queue = task_queue

    async def run(self):
        while True:
            task = await self.task_queue.get()
            try:
                await self.process(task)
            finally:
                self.task_queue.task_done()

    async def process(self, task):
        # Simulate asynchronous task processing
        await asyncio.sleep(task['duration'])
        print(f"Processed task {task['id']}")

async def main():
    task_queue = Queue()

    # Start multiple workers
    workers = [Worker(task_queue) for _ in range(3)]
    worker_tasks = [asyncio.create_task(worker.run()) for worker
    in workers]

    # Enqueue some tasks
    for i in range(10):
        await task_queue.put({'id': i, 'duration': 0.5})
```

```
    await task_queue.join()  # Wait until all tasks are processed

    for w in worker_tasks:
        w.cancel()

asyncio.run(main())
```

```
Processed task 0
Processed task 1
Processed task 2
Processed task 3
Processed task 4
Processed task 5
Processed task 6
Processed task 7
Processed task 8
Processed task 9
```

This pattern demonstrates several core aspects:

- **Decoupling**: Task producers and workers operate independently without blocking.

- **Concurrency**:   Multiple   workers   process   tasks
  concurrently, increasing throughput.

- **Backpressure and Flow Control**: The queue naturally
  buffers incoming tasks, avoiding overload.

- **Asynchronous I/O**: Using `asyncio` allows cooperative
  multitasking without blocking threads.

In real-world systems, message queues may extend over multiple
processes or machines, and actors encapsulate more complex state
and behaviors.

By designing systems that communicate asynchronously through
message queues and actor-based patterns, engineers can build
highly responsive interfaces that remain reactive under load without thread starvation or blocking waits. Moreover, background

processing tasks can scale horizontally by adding more consumers or actor instances without changing business logic, affording elasticity critical to modern cloud-native applications.

The inherent decoupling also enhances fault tolerance: failures in one component do not cascade immediately because messages may remain queued or retried according to policy. Moreover, monitoring and instrumentation become more straightforward by observing message flows and queue depths.

Leveraging message queues combined with asynchronous programming techniques such as the actor model provides a robust foundation for building scalable, resilient, and responsive software systems capable of meeting demanding concurrency and availability requirements.

6.4. Thread-safe Data Structures

In multi-threaded applications, data integrity and consistency are paramount. Shared data structures accessed simultaneously by multiple threads must be designed carefully to avoid race conditions, deadlocks, and other concurrency hazards. Delphi provides multiple mechanisms and paradigms to create thread-safe data structures, focusing particularly on concurrent collections and lock-free programming. This section explores their foundational principles, implementation techniques, and best practices in Delphi environments.

Concurrent collections serve as the cornerstone for managing shared state in multi-threaded scenarios. Unlike traditional collections susceptible to corruption under concurrent access, concurrent collections implement synchronization internally to ensure thread safety. Delphi's RTL (Run-Time Library) includes thread-safe wrappers for many common data structures, but to fully leverage multi-core processors and minimize bottlenecks, more sophisticated approaches like lock-free programming become essential.

Thread safety in data structures fundamentally requires controlling access so that concurrent operations do not interfere destructively. Two broad paradigms dominate this effort:

- **Lock-based synchronization:** Uses mutual exclusion primitives such as critical sections, mutexes, or monitors to serialize access. Although simple and widely used, locking can cause contention, priority inversion, and even deadlocks if not managed correctly.

- **Lock-free synchronization:** Employs atomic operations and memory barriers to guarantee data consistency without explicit locks. This approach reduces overhead and improves scalability but requires careful design and understanding of hardware memory models.

Lock-free data structures rely on atomic read-modify-write operations like Compare-And-Swap (CAS), InterlockedIncrement, InterlockedCompareExchange, and similar primitives available in Delphi's System unit.

Delphi RTL provides the `TThreadList` and `TThreadQueue` classes as basic synchronized collections. For example, TThreadList encapsulates a `TList` and guards it via an internal critical section to serialize access:

```
var
  ThreadList: TThreadList<Integer>;
  ListSnapshot: TList<Integer>;
  Item: Integer;
begin
  ThreadList := TThreadList<Integer>.Create;
  try
    ThreadList.Add(10);
    ThreadList.Add(20);
    ListSnapshot := ThreadList.LockList;
    try
      for Item in ListSnapshot do
```

```
      // Process items safely
  finally
    ThreadList.UnlockList;
  end;
finally
  ThreadList.Free;
end;
end;
```

While effective, such coarse-grained locking can limit parallelism under high contention. Thus, the design and usage of collections must balance ease-of-use, safety, and performance.

Delphi's System.Generics.Collections include TQueue<T> and TStack<T> but lack intrinsic synchronization. To overcome this, modern Delphi versions enable lock-free queue implementations or offer thread-safe variants through third-party libraries or custom solutions.

Lock-free programming in Delphi involves designing algorithms and structures that guarantee progress among threads without requiring blocking synchronization. Proper implementations avoid common pitfalls such as ABA problems, memory reclamation issues, or subtle ordering bugs.

Atomic Operations and Memory Barriers

Delphi's System.SyncObjs and System units provide atomic functions critical for lock-free structures:

- InterlockedCompareExchange atomically compares a memory location with a given comparator value and, if equal, updates it to a new value.

- InterlockedIncrement/InterlockedDecrement atomically add or subtract from an integer.

These atomic primitives ensure that concurrent updates cannot interleave destructively, preserving data integrity.

Designing Lock-free Queues

Consider a single-producer, single-consumer (SPSC) queue implemented without explicit locks. This approach can achieve very high throughput, suitable for producer-consumer scenarios common in high-performance systems.

One practical implementation employs a fixed-size circular buffer with two atomic indices: Head (read position) and Tail (write position). The producer advances Tail atomically, and the consumer advances Head atomically, with appropriate memory barriers to avoid reordering issues.

```
type
  TLockFreeSPSCQueue = class
  private
    Buffer: array of Integer;
    Head, Tail: Integer; // Int32 indices
    SizeMask: Integer;
  public
    constructor Create(Capacity: Integer);
    function Enqueue(const Value: Integer): Boolean;
    function Dequeue(out Value: Integer): Boolean;
  end;

constructor TLockFreeSPSCQueue.Create(Capacity: Integer);
begin
  // Capacity must be power of two for mask
  SetLength(Buffer, Capacity);
  SizeMask := Capacity - 1;
  Head := 0;
  Tail := 0;
end;

function TLockFreeSPSCQueue.Enqueue(const Value: Integer):
    Boolean;
var
  NextTail: Integer;
begin
  NextTail := (Tail + 1) and SizeMask;
  if NextTail = Head then
    Exit(False);   // Queue is full
  Buffer[Tail] := Value;
  // Memory barrier implied by InterlockedCompareExchange
  Tail := NextTail;
  Result := True;
end;

function TLockFreeSPSCQueue.Dequeue(out Value: Integer): Boolean;
begin
  if Head = Tail then
```

```
   Exit(False);  // Queue empty
 Value := Buffer[Head];
 Head := (Head + 1) and SizeMask;
 Result := True;
end;
```

Although simplified, this lock-free pattern provides significant performance gains over mutex-based queues when used in appropriate contexts, especially when matched to CPU cache lines and avoiding false sharing.

Dealing with Complex Lock-free Structures

Extending lock-free programming to multiple producers and consumers (MPMC queues) or complex collections demands advanced techniques such as hazard pointers or epoch-based memory reclamation, which prevent reclaiming objects still accessible by other threads. While Delphi's RTL does not natively provide these mechanisms, they can be implemented or sourced through community libraries. The foundational understanding of atomic primitives remains crucial for such endeavors.

Effective design of concurrent data structures in Delphi should adhere to the following principles:

- **Favor immutability where possible:** Immutable data requires no synchronization and simplifies reasoning.

- **Minimize shared mutable state:** Isolate state per thread if feasible, reducing contention.

- **Encapsulate synchronization internally:** Public APIs should provide thread-safe interfaces hiding low-level concurrency details.

- **Choose the appropriate synchronization strategy:** Use locks for low-contention or simple scenarios. Prefer lock-free for high-throughput, contention-prone components.

- **Validate correctness rigorously:** Concurrency bugs are notoriously elusive. Unit tests and formal methods can help ensure robustness.

A common concurrent data structure is a thread-safe dictionary. Delphi does not provide a built-in one; thus, developers often extend TDictionary<TKey, TValue> with synchronization.

A simple approach uses a read-write lock around dictionary operations:

```
type
  TThreadSafeDictionary<TKey, TValue> = class
  private
    FDictionary: TDictionary<TKey, TValue>;
    FRWLock: TMultiReadExclusiveWriteSynchronizer;
  public
    constructor Create;
    destructor Destroy; override;
    procedure AddOrSetValue(const Key: TKey; const Value: TValue)
     ;
    function TryGetValue(const Key: TKey; out Value: TValue):
     Boolean;
    procedure Remove(const Key: TKey);
  end;

constructor TThreadSafeDictionary<TKey, TValue>.Create;
begin
  inherited;
  FDictionary := TDictionary<TKey, TValue>.Create;
  FRWLock := TMultiReadExclusiveWriteSynchronizer.Create;
end;

destructor TThreadSafeDictionary<TKey, TValue>.Destroy;
begin
  FRWLock.Free;
  FDictionary.Free;
  inherited;
end;

procedure TThreadSafeDictionary<TKey, TValue>.AddOrSetValue(const
     Key: TKey; const Value: TValue);
begin
  FRWLock.BeginWrite;
  try
    FDictionary.AddOrSetValue(Key, Value);
  finally
    FRWLock.EndWrite;
  end;
```

150

```
end;

function TThreadSafeDictionary<TKey, TValue>.TryGetValue(const
    Key: TKey; out Value: TValue): Boolean;
begin
  FRWLock.BeginRead;
  try
    Result := FDictionary.TryGetValue(Key, Value);
  finally
    FRWLock.EndRead;
  end;
end;

procedure TThreadSafeDictionary<TKey, TValue>.Remove(const Key:
    TKey);
begin
  FRWLock.BeginWrite;
  try
    FDictionary.Remove(Key);
  finally
    FRWLock.EndWrite;
  end;
end;
```

This implementation allows multiple readers concurrently while exclusive writers block readers and other writers, balancing performance and safety for typical dictionary usage patterns.

Thread-safe data structures in Delphi require a blending of low-level atomic operations and high-level synchronization abstractions tailored to the application's concurrency patterns and performance goals. Lock-based collections serve as accessible starting points, while lock-free designs offer lower latency and improved scalability for demanding applications. Understanding the underlying hardware and memory models, combined with rigorous testing, ensures robust and efficient use of concurrent data structures.

This foundation supports writing maintainable and high-performance multi-threaded applications in Delphi, enabling safe evolution of complex systems leveraging modern multicore processors.

6.5. Performance Optimization for Parallel Code

Efficient parallel code execution necessitates a rigorous approach to profiling, analyzing, and tuning workloads to fully exploit available hardware resources. Profiling tools enable identification of performance bottlenecks, guiding efforts to enhance throughput and resource utilization. This section addresses critical strategies for maximizing CPU utilization, mitigating contention, and harnessing architectural features for accelerated parallel performance.

Profiling Parallel Workloads

Profiling is a foundational step in performance optimization. Unlike serial code, parallel applications introduce complexities such as thread synchronization, workload imbalance, and memory contention. Profilers specialized for concurrency, such as `Intel VTune`, `perf`, and `gprof`, offer metrics beyond CPU cycles, including thread-level execution details, cache misses, and contention rates.

Key metrics to extract during profiling include:

- **CPU Utilization**: Measures how effectively threads saturate CPU cores.

- **Load Imbalance**: Disparity in work distribution among parallel units leading to idle times.

- **Synchronization Overhead**: Time spent on locks, barriers, or atomic operations.

- **Memory Access Patterns**: Cache hit/miss ratios and latency due to non-uniform memory access (NUMA).

Interpreting these metrics allows for targeted interventions, such as rebalancing workloads or restructuring synchronization mechanisms.

Maximizing CPU Utilization

Achieving near-peak CPU utilization requires both algorithmic and systemic considerations. Over-subscription of threads can cause context switching overhead, while under-utilization results in idle core time. A common approach employs thread pools sized in accordance with the number of physical or logical cores, avoiding oversubscribing which tends to degrade performance due to increased scheduling delays.

Task granularity directly impacts CPU utilization. Fine-grained tasks improve load balancing but increase scheduling overhead; conversely, coarse-grained tasks reduce overhead but may lead to imbalance. Techniques such as work-stealing schedulers dynamically redistribute tasks, mitigating idle times without excessive overhead.

Additionally, minimizing synchronization delays is paramount. Lock contention can serialize portions of parallel work, negating the benefits of concurrency. Use of lock-free data structures, reduction operations, or employing atomic primitives judiciously can reduce such contention.

Minimizing Contention and Synchronization Overhead

Contention arises primarily from concurrent access to shared resources. Identifying contention hotspots is critical; profiling tools that report lock wait times and false sharing incidents serve instrumental roles.

False sharing occurs when threads modify variables located on the same cache line, triggering unnecessary cache coherence traffic. Aligning frequently modified variables on separate cache lines (for instance, via padding or compiler-specific attributes) mitigates this problem.

When synchronization is unavoidable, consider alternatives to traditional locks:

- **Spinlocks** provide low-latency locks ideal for short critical sections but consume CPU cycles while spinning.

- **Read-Write Locks** allow multiple concurrent readers but exclusive writers, reducing contention when reads dominate.

- **Lock-Free Algorithms** utilize atomic operations to avoid locking entirely, often leading to superior scalability.

Barrier synchronization should be minimized, and where necessary, algorithms like hierarchical or asynchronous barriers can reduce the associated latency.

Exploiting Hardware Capabilities

Modern CPUs provide several hardware features to accelerate parallel computation. Awareness and utilization of these features are critical to performance optimization.

SIMD Vectorization

Single Instruction, Multiple Data (SIMD) units enable simultaneous operations on multiple data points. Compilers often auto-vectorize loops, but explicit vectorization via intrinsics or specialized libraries can yield superior results, especially in compute-heavy kernels. Aligning data for vector access and minimizing branching within vectorized code are important considerations.

NUMA Awareness

Non-Uniform Memory Access architectures demand careful memory allocation and thread affinity management. Ensuring that threads access memory local to their NUMA node reduces latency significantly. Operating system APIs and runtime libraries often support NUMA-aware allocation and scheduling.

Hardware Prefetching and Cache Utilization

Optimal data access patterns improve cache hit rates and leverage hardware prefetchers. Prefetch instructions or compiler directives can hint the processor to load data ahead of time. Structuring data in arrays of structures versus structures of arrays impacts spatial locality and cache behavior, thus affecting performance.

Example: Profiling and Tuning a Parallel Matrix Multiplication

Consider a parallel matrix multiplication coded with OpenMP. Initial profiling reveals that although CPU utilization is high, a significant fraction of time is spent in synchronization barriers and memory stalls.

A sample code snippet:

```
#pragma omp parallel for schedule(static)
for (int i = 0; i < N; i++) {
    for (int j = 0; j < N; j++) {
        double sum = 0.0;
        for (int k = 0; k < N; k++) {
            sum += A[i][k] * B[k][j];
        }
        C[i][j] = sum;
    }
}
```

Profiling output shows load imbalance due to static scheduling and high memory bandwidth usage.

To improve utilization and reduce contention, schedule dynamic work distribution with chunk sizes optimized through experimentation:

```
#pragma omp parallel for schedule(dynamic, 16)
for (int i = 0; i < N; i++) {
    ...
}
```

Tuning data layouts for cache efficiency by blocking (tiling) reduces cache misses and improves memory locality:

```
int blockSize = 64;
for (int i0 = 0; i0 < N; i0 += blockSize) {
    for (int j0 = 0; j0 < N; j0 += blockSize) {
```

155

```
for (int k0 = 0; k0 < N; k0 += blockSize) {
    for (int i = i0; i < min(i0 + blockSize, N); i++) {
        for (int j = j0; j < min(j0 + blockSize, N); j++)
{
            double sum = 0.0;
            for (int k = k0; k < min(k0 + blockSize, N);
k++) {
                sum += A[i][k] * B[k][j];
            }
            C[i][j] += sum;
        }
    }
}
}
```

Benchmarking after these changes typically shows reduced synchronization overhead, better load balance, and improved cache utilization, leading to up to several-fold speedups.

Summary of Best Practices

- Profile early and often, focusing on metrics that reveal load imbalance, synchronization overhead, and memory bottlenecks.

- Tune thread counts and scheduling policies to align with hardware core counts and workload characteristics.

- Minimize synchronization and contention by applying lock-free techniques, padding to avoid false sharing, and reducing critical section length.

- Leverage hardware features such as SIMD instructions, NUMA-aware allocations, and cache-friendly data layouts.

- Employ algorithmic optimizations like work stealing, task granularity adjustments, and blocking for cache efficiency.

Mastering the interplay between software parallel constructs and hardware resources lays the foundation for extracting maximal performance from parallel applications.

6.6. Deadlock Detection and Debugging

Deadlock conditions in concurrent systems arise when multiple threads become permanently blocked, each waiting for resources held by others. Such scenarios degrade performance and can halt system progress, making their detection and resolution critical in advanced multi-threaded application development. This section examines sophisticated methods for diagnosing thread contention issues, approaches for identifying and resolving deadlocks, and explores Delphi's integrated debugging tools tailored for complex thread interactions.

Detecting deadlocks begins with understanding the system's resource allocation graph (RAG). Here, vertices represent threads and resources, and edges capture ownership and waiting relationships. A cycle in this graph signifies a deadlock. Automated detection thus involves constructing this graph dynamically during execution and periodically performing cycle detection algorithms. Using data structures like adjacency lists combined with depth-first search (DFS) or Tarjan's strongly connected components algorithm provides efficient detection, even in systems with numerous threads and resources.

Thread contention, a precursor to deadlock, can also be diagnosed through profiling locks' acquisition patterns and durations. Recording timestamps and thread identifiers at lock requests allows the identification of hotspots where threads are frequently blocked. These profiles inform whether lock granularity needs adjustment or if redesigning mutual exclusion strategies (e.g., upgrading from coarse-grained to fine-grained locks) could mitigate contention.

Delphi's multi-threaded debugging environment offers comprehensive tools to capture and analyze such behaviors. The Thread Status Window displays active threads, their current states, call stacks, and synchronization primitives they are waiting on or holding. This real-time view assists in pinpointing the exact resource or lock causing a thread's suspension. Integrating this with the Event Log can highlight repetitive patterns of blocking or spinning, beneficial for tracing the progression towards deadlock conditions.

An advanced approach involves implementing custom diagnostic instrumentation in code. Hooks placed around lock acquisition and release points emit detailed trace logs, capturing the time, thread identity, resource ID, and call context. These logs can be parsed post-execution or streamed to tools for live analysis. Below is an illustrative example applying such instrumentation for a critical section protected by a TCriticalSection object:

```
procedure AcquireLockAndLog(CS: TCriticalSection; const
    ResourceID: string);
begin
  LogEvent(Format('Thread %d requesting lock %s at %s', [
    GetCurrentThreadId, ResourceID, DateTimeToStr(Now)]));
  CS.Enter;
  LogEvent(Format('Thread %d acquired lock %s at %s', [
    GetCurrentThreadId, ResourceID, DateTimeToStr(Now)]));
end;

procedure ReleaseLockAndLog(CS: TCriticalSection; const
    ResourceID: string);
begin
  LogEvent(Format('Thread %d releasing lock %s at %s', [
    GetCurrentThreadId, ResourceID, DateTimeToStr(Now)]));
  CS.Leave;
end;
```

These logs can be analyzed to observe lock hold times and potential circular wait patterns. They also provide breadcrumbs for post-mortem deadlock analysis.

When a deadlock is suspected, the Delphi Debugger allows freezing the application and examining all threads' call stacks simultaneously. By inspecting the synchronization objects each thread is waiting for, developers can reconstruct the wait-for graph manually. Tools such as the integrated Threads view provide direct insight into thread states like Waiting, Terminated, or Running, and their blocking conditions.

Resolving detected deadlocks typically involves breaking the circular wait condition by imposing strict lock acquisition ordering policies. For instance, globally ordering resources and requiring threads to acquire locks in ascending sequence prevents cyclic dependencies. Alternatively, employing try-lock mechanisms with timeout detection enables threads to back off and retry, thus avoiding indefinite blockage.

Advanced debugger features in Delphi also support conditional breakpoints that activate only when threads attempt to acquire locks already held by other threads, triggering on specific contention scenarios. This conditional breakpoint assists in early detection and dynamic investigation without freezing simpler concurrent operations.

Furthermore, analyzing deadlocks in event-driven or asynchronous paradigms requires attention to message queues and synchronization contexts. Delphi's tools for inspecting TTask and synchronization context objects reveal subtle interaction deadlocks invisible in classical locking analysis.

Kernel-level diagnostic tools complement Delphi's IDE by providing lower-level thread and synchronization state inspection. Windows Performance Analyzer (WPA) and Debugging Tools for Windows (WinDbg), used in tandem with Delphi, allow tracing kernel waits and lock ownership across process boundaries, enhancing deadlock detection in distributed or multi-process environments.

Effective diagnosis of thread contention and deadlock involves a combination of algorithmic graph analysis, logging-based instrumentation, and meticulous examination using advanced debugging tools. Delphi's integrated environment equips developers with tailored views, conditional breakpoints, and thread status exploration, forming a robust toolkit to analyze and resolve complex multi-threaded behaviors. Adopting strict lock ordering, leveraging timeout strategies, and incrementally refining synchronization designs based on comprehensive diagnostics significantly enhances application robustness against deadlocks.

Chapter 7

Testing, Debugging, and Quality Assurance

Beyond delivering software that works, Delphi developers must ensure applications are robust, reliable, and maintainable. This chapter unveils advanced methodologies and tooling that transform raw code into thoroughly tested, finely tuned, and confidently shipped solutions. Elevate your development lifecycle through comprehensive testing, strategic debugging, and rigorous quality assurance practices.

7.1. Advanced Unit Testing with DUnitX

DUnitX extends the fundamental capabilities of Delphi unit testing frameworks by providing a powerful and flexible environment for designing expressive, maintainable, and comprehensive test suites. This section delves into advanced techniques to master unit testing using DUnitX, focusing on sophisticated test design patterns, the effective use of mocks and stubs, systematic management of test data, and the formulation of expressive assertions that capture intricate behavioral expectations.

When writing unit tests, structuring test cases with clarity and efficiency is critical to scalability and maintenance. DUnitX supports a variety of test organization strategies beyond simple method-based tests. Key among these is the use of Setup and TearDown methods, which prepare the environment before each test and clean up afterward, ensuring test independence and avoiding side effects:

```
type
  TMyComponentTests = class(TObject)
  private
    FComponent: TMyComponent;
  public
    [Setup]
    procedure Setup;
    [TearDown]
    procedure TearDown;
  published
    procedure TestInitialization;
    procedure TestOperation;
  end;

procedure TMyComponentTests.Setup;
begin
  FComponent := TMyComponent.Create;
  // Additional setup code here
end;

procedure TMyComponentTests.TearDown;
begin
  FComponent.Free;
  // Additional cleanup code here
end;
```

By encapsulating repetitive setup and teardown logic, tests are less error-prone and easier to read. Moreover, DUnitX supports *parameterized tests* using TestCase attributes to run the same test logic against diverse input values efficiently:

```
procedure TestAddition;
begin
  Assert.AreEqual(Expected, Calculator.Add(Arg1, Arg2));
end;

[TestCase('AddPositives', '2,3,5')]
[TestCase('AddNegatives', '-1,-2,-3')]
```

```
[TestCase('AddMixed', '5,-3,2')]
procedure TCalculatorTests.TestAddition(const Arg1, Arg2,
    Expected: Integer);
```

This approach improves test coverage with minimal code duplication and maintains clear mapping between inputs and expected outputs.

Creating isolated test environments often involves replacing dependencies with controlled substitutes. DUnitX integrates seamlessly with third-party mocking frameworks such as Delphi Mocks, enhancing the ability to simulate complex interactions without relying on actual implementations. Mocks can verify that methods are called with expected parameters, while stubs return controlled data.

Example usage of Delphi Mocks within DUnitX demonstrates this concept:

```
uses
  Delphi.Mocks;

type
  IDataService = interface
    function GetData(id: Integer): string;
  end;

procedure TServiceTests.TestProcessData;
var
  MockDataService: TMock<IDataService>;
  Service: TMyService;
begin
  MockDataService := TMock<IDataService>.Create;
  MockDataService.Setup.WillReturn('MockedData').When.GetData(42)
    ;

  Service := TMyService.Create(MockDataService.Instance);
  try
    Service.ProcessData(42);
    // Verify interaction
    MockDataService.Received(1).GetData(42);
  finally
    Service.Free;
  end;
end;
```

Stubs, by contrast, provide fixed responses without behavioral verification, suited for simpler scenarios. Mastering the distinction between mocks and stubs enables precise control over test dependencies and promotes the principle of testing units in isolation.

Reliable testing requires consistent and representative test data. DUnitX tests benefit from thoughtful strategies for organizing and injecting data, reducing brittleness and enhancing clarity. Common patterns for test data management include:

- **Inline constants and arrays**: Suitable for small sets of input-output pairs expressed via TestCase attributes.

- **Data provider methods**: Return dynamic collections of test scenarios, enabling complex or computed datasets.

- **External data sources**: Read from JSON, XML, or database files to manage large or shared datasets, improving separation of concerns.

An example of data-driven testing through a data provider method is:

```
type
  TCalculatorTests = class(TObject)
  published
    [Test]
    [TestCaseSource('AddTestCases')]
    procedure TestAddition(const Arg1, Arg2, Expected: Integer);
  public
    class function AddTestCases: TArray<TTestCaseData>;
  end;

class function TCalculatorTests.AddTestCases: TArray<
    TTestCaseData>;
begin
  Result := TArray<TTestCaseData>.Create(
    TTestCaseData.Create('Test1', [2, 3, 5]),
    TTestCaseData.Create('Test2', [-1, -2, -3]),
    TTestCaseData.Create('Test3', [10, 15, 25])
  );
end;
```

Such abstractions permit the independent evolution of test logic and data, accommodate scaling, and facilitate collaboration.

Assertions form the backbone of unit tests, capturing the criteria used to declare success or failure. While DUnitX provides a rich set of built-in assertions such as `AreEqual`, `IsTrue`, `IsNotNull`, and various exception verifications, advanced testing demands precise and descriptive assertions to enhance diagnostic output and reduce debugging time.

Expressive assertions improve clarity and communicate intent more effectively. Examples include:

```
Assert.WillNotRaise(procedure begin
  FComponent.MethodUnderTest;
end);

Assert.WillRaiseWithMessage(EArgumentException, 'Invalid
    parameter', procedure begin
  FComponent.MethodUnderTest(-1);
end);

Assert.AreEqual<Currency>(ExpectedValue, ActualValue, 0.0001, '
    Unexpected currency result');
```

Custom assertions can be implemented by extending `TAssert` or by creating helper methods to encapsulate domain-specific verification logic. For instance:

```
class procedure TAssert.AssertIsValidUser(const User: TUser);
begin
  Assert.IsNotNull(User, 'User instance should not be nil');
  Assert.IsTrue(User.IsActive, 'User must be active');
  Assert.IsNotEmpty(User.Email, 'User email must be set');
end;

procedure TUserTests.TestUserValidation;
begin
  var User := TUser.Create;
  User.IsActive := True;
  User.Email := 'user@example.com';
  try
    TAssert.AssertIsValidUser(User);
  finally
    User.Free;
  end;
end;
```

This construct fosters reuse and improves test readability by abstracting complex assertions into semantic units.

Unit testing aims to validate the smallest testable parts of an application, typically individual classes or methods, ensuring deterministic and isolated verification of logic. Combining advanced test design, controlled dependency injection through mocks and stubs, careful organization of test data, and finely tuned assertions leads to thorough and robust test suites.

DUnitX supports parallel test execution and test fixtures at various granularities, which, coupled with its extensible reporting and continuous integration compatibility, creates a professional-grade testing environment. The strategic application of these advanced techniques fortifies code reliability by detecting regressions early, clarifying design assumptions, and embodying executable documentation within development workflows.

By mastering these aspects of DUnitX, developers achieve not only higher test precision and coverage but also foster maintainable and fast feedback cycles essential to high-quality Delphi software engineering.

7.2. Integration, System, and UI Testing

Testing beyond individual units is essential to ensure correct functionality when components interact within a Delphi application. Integration testing focuses on verifying inter-module communication and data exchange, system testing addresses the application as a whole in an environment approximating production, and UI testing validates user interaction flows, which is especially critical in the complex graphical environments typical of Delphi applications.

Integration testing begins after unit testing confirms isolated components perform as expected. Unlike isolated units, integration tests expose interface inconsistencies, incorrect assumptions about data formats, and timing issues in asynchronous communication. In Delphi applications, integration tests frequently target interactions between forms, data modules, and business logic layers. Test harnesses should simulate real communication patterns and verify expected outcomes, emphasizing boundary and error conditions in data flow. For example, when a data module supplies datasets consumed by multiple forms, integration tests verify that changes in underlying data trigger appropriate UI updates without introducing race conditions.

Structured strategies such as top-down, bottom-up, and sandwich integration testing remain relevant. Top-down integration employs stubs to simulate lower-level modules, enabling early verification of high-level interactions and workflows. Bottom-up testing uses drivers to facilitate early testing of foundational modules before the entire system is available. Sandwich integration combines both approaches for comprehensive coverage. In Delphi, leveraging runtime packages and modular design facilitates isolating subsystems for targeted integration testing. The Delphi IDE's debugging and live inspection support aid in tracing intercomponent calls and state changes during integration tests.

System testing validates the fully integrated application in an environment closely reflecting production configurations, including databases, network services, and hardware interfaces. This level of testing often uses automated or manual end-to-end scenarios assessing functional requirements, performance benchmarks, security constraints, and interoperability. Since system tests encompass broad application behavior, test cases are designed from user stories and specification requirements, ensuring coverage of realistic workflows rather than isolated operations. External dependencies are generally deployed or mocked with high fidelity to minimize false positives or negatives related to environment discrepancies.

Automation frameworks for system testing in Delphi commonly integrate command-line test executions and scripting engines to control test execution and gather metrics. Continuous Integration (CI) pipelines can orchestrate system test runs on various deployments, ensuring rapid feedback on new builds. Logging and monitoring components embedded within the application assist in correlating test failures with runtime events, minimizing diagnosis time.

User Interface (UI) testing in Delphi applications presents particular challenges due to highly interactive, event-driven paradigms. Manual UI testing is laborious and error-prone, necessitating automation to handle regression testing and frequent UI changes. Automated UI testing tools interact with visual components, simulating user actions such as clicks, data entry, and drag-and-drop operations. Tools like TestComplete, Ranorex, or open-source alternatives can interface with the Delphi VCL and FireMonkey controls through accessible properties, object hierarchies, and event hooks.

Key techniques for robust UI testing include object recognition based on stable properties (e.g., control names, identifiers) rather than screen coordinates, enabling tests to remain valid through layout modifications. Test scripts are best organized to mimic user scenarios, incorporating waits and synchronization to handle asynchronous UI updates and background operations. Assertions focus on the presence, properties, and state of UI elements after interaction sequences to validate correctness.

Delphi's own testing ecosystem can complement UI automation with specialized libraries such as DUnitX, which allow integrating unit and integration tests with high-level UI tests by exposing test hooks in the application code. Custom interfaces or auxiliary test forms can automate commonly required UI states, reducing the complexity of scripting rare or difficult interactions.

An increasingly effective approach is adopting Model-View-Presenter (MVP) or Model-View-ViewModel (MVVM) architectural patterns to decouple UI logic from visual elements, enhancing testability. By isolating presentation logic in testable units, much functional verification can shift from brittle UI tests to more stable unit and integration tests. This layered separation reduces overall test maintenance effort and improves reliability, especially in large-scale Delphi applications with complex user interfaces.

A practical example of automated UI interaction validation in Delphi can use the UIAutomation COM interfaces available in Windows to programmatically manipulate and query standard UI components. Integration with scripting languages like Python or PowerShell expedites writing versatile test scripts that interact with the Delphi application at the UI level, validating workflows such as data input, navigation through dialogs, and error message handling.

Consider the following simplified Delphi pseudocode illustrating a method for triggering UI validation and capturing testable state after a simulated user action:

```
procedure TFormMain.TestInputAndValidate;
begin
  EditUsername.Text := 'testuser';
  EditPassword.Text := 'password123';
  BtnLogin.Click;

  // Await asynchronous login operation completion
  while LoadingSpinner.Visible do
    Application.ProcessMessages;

  Assert(LabelStatus.Caption = 'Login successful', 'Login failed
    or incorrect status message');
end;
```

Automating repetitive UI tests accelerates feedback loops and increases coverage confidence, which is crucial when evolving complex Delphi applications with extensive user interactions. Nevertheless, UI test automation must be supplemented by comprehensive integration and system tests to ensure all interfaces and subsystems collectively perform as intended.

An effective testing strategy beyond units in Delphi applications involves coordinated approaches to integration, system, and UI tests. Utilizing modular design principles, automation frameworks, and architectural decoupling enhances test robustness and maintainability. These strategies collectively establish high assurance in complex application correctness, performance, and usability across evolving development cycles.

7.3. Debugging Complex Applications

In complex software systems—particularly those that are large-scale, distributed, or performance-critical—debugging becomes a nontrivial task that requires a disciplined approach and specialized tools. Delphi's integrated development environment (IDE) provides an extensive suite of debugging facilities tailored to aid developers in dissecting and resolving such intricate issues. These facilities include advanced breakpoints, watch expressions, symbol management, and remote debugging capabilities, each playing a pivotal role in navigating and understanding program behavior under difficult conditions.

Breakpoints in Delphi offer far more than simple code execution halting. Conditional breakpoints can suspend execution only when specific runtime conditions are met—variables reach certain values or program states occur—reducing the overhead of manual inspection. Tracepoint breakpoints extend this concept by logging information without stopping execution, enabling unobtrusive insight into code paths and variable states during high-demand performance scenarios. The configuration of breakpoints supports hit counts, allowing developers to halt after a breakpoint is passed a precise number of times, facilitating the capture of intermittent or rare bugs.

Watch expressions form a cornerstone for monitoring critical variables or expressions dynamically throughout program execution.

In Delphi, watches can be specified to evaluate complex expressions or object properties at each step without explicit output statements in source code. When working with distributed applications where internal states are fragmented across modules or threads, strategically placed watch expressions permit the developer to track the evolution of data as it propagates through the system. Watches combined with breakpoints offer a powerful synergy, enabling conditional watches that only update when certain breakpoints trigger, streamlining the debugging workflow significantly.

Symbol management is fundamental when dealing with large applications, especially those composed of multiple packages or dynamically loaded modules. Delphi generates comprehensive debug symbol files (.tds) containing metadata such as function addresses, variable locations, and line number mappings. Proper management of these symbol files ensures that the debugger can accurately correlate runtime data to source code, a necessity for meaningful stack traces and step-through debugging. In distributed systems, symbol files must be deployed alongside the binaries on remote machines or test environments to maintain full debugging functionality. Misaligned or missing symbols typically result in obscured call stacks or the inability to inspect variables, complicating root-cause analysis.

Remote debugging capabilities in Delphi elevate the effectiveness of diagnosing problems in software running on distinct hardware or isolated environments such as embedded devices, virtual machines, or cloud servers. By establishing a remote debugger session via IP connection or debug server interfaces, developers gain full access to the target process, including the ability to manipulate breakpoints, inspect state, and control execution flow as if running locally. This is indispensable for performance-critical applications where reproducing timing or load conditions on a local machine is impractical. Remote debugging also facilitates the investigation of issues related to network latency, interprocess communication, or environment-specific behavior that only manifest outside the development container.

Combining these features requires deliberate setup and under-standing. The debugger's ability to attach to running processes enables on-the-fly investigation of crashes or hang states without restarting the application, essential for minimizing system down-time during analysis. Particularly, in multi-threaded or paral-lelized code, thread-aware debugging tools help identify race con-ditions and deadlocks by providing a thread list, call stacks per thread, and synchronization object states. Utilizing breakpoints with thread-specific filtering avoids excessive interruption, allow-ing focus on the particular thread where the bug manifests.

Performance profiling tools, while not strictly part of the debugger, complement the debugging process by highlighting bottlenecks and ineffective code paths that may contribute indirectly to faults or degraded responsiveness. Integrating profiling insights with breakpoints and watches allows narrowing down problems corre-lated with metrics such as CPU usage, memory consumption, and execution time.

An example of configuring a conditional breakpoint and watch ex-pression in Delphi's debugger is as follows:

```
procedure TMyForm.ButtonClick(Sender: TObject);
var
  Counter: Integer;
begin
  Counter := 0;
  while Counter < 100 do
  begin
    Inc(Counter);
    if Counter = 42 then
      ShowMessage('The answer');

    // Breakpoint set here with condition: Counter > 40
    // Watch expression set for 'Counter' variable
  end;
end;
```

Using the debugger, the breakpoint would only trigger when Counter exceeds 40, minimizing unnecessary stops.

172

Simultaneously, the watch expression monitors `Counter`, allowing continuous visibility into its value evolution.

Ultimately, mastering Delphi's debugging facilities requires combining foundational techniques—such as setting breakpoints and watches—with advanced capabilities like remote debugging, symbolic information coordination, and thread visualization. This comprehensive toolkit empowers developers to penetrate the opacity of complex software systems and systematically identify, analyze, and resolve defects, even in the most challenging environments.

7.4. Profiling Tools and Performance Analysis

Performance optimization requires precise identification of bottlenecks and anomalies within an application's execution flow. Profiling tools are essential for discovering *hot paths*—the most frequently executed and time-consuming sections of code—detecting *memory leaks*, and diagnosing *race conditions*. Both managed environments, such as those running on virtual machines with garbage collection, and native codebases, which operate closer to hardware, demand tailored profiling strategies to uncover inefficiencies and concurrency issues.

Identifying Hot Paths and Bottlenecks

Hot path analysis focuses on determining which functions or lines of code dominate runtime behavior. Sampling profilers intermittently capture the program counter, assembling a statistical view of code execution frequencies without significantly perturbing program flow. In contrast, instrumentation-based profilers insert timing hooks around functions or code blocks to obtain precise execution counts and durations at the cost of higher overhead.

For native applications, tools such as `perf` on Linux or Intel VTune Profiler utilize hardware performance counters to measure CPU cycles, cache misses, and branch mispredictions linked to code segments. These data assist in pinpointing *computationally intensive* routines. In managed runtimes like the Java Virtual Machine (JVM) or .NET CLR, profilers such as VisualVM, YourKit, or dotTrace provide flame graphs and method-level timing, integrating with garbage collection and JIT compiler activity for accurate correlation.

```
perf record -F 99 -p <pid> -g -- sleep 30
perf report
```

Here, `perf record` captures stack traces at a 99 Hz sampling frequency for 30 seconds on the process with PID <pid>, then `perf report` visualizes the hot paths.

Flame graphs, introduced by Brendan Gregg, visually represent hierarchical profiling data, with wider blocks indicating heavier time consumption. They succinctly reveal which call chains dominate CPU time, enabling developers to target optimization efforts effectively.

Memory Leak Detection

Memory leaks occur when allocated memory is no longer referenced yet remains unfreed, gradually exhausting available memory and potentially causing performance degradation or crashes. In managed environments equipped with garbage collectors, leaks often result from unintended object retention due to lingering references. In native code, leaks manifest as failure to call `free()`, `delete`, or similar routines on allocated resources.

Profiling tools specialized in memory analysis provide heap snapshots, allocation call stacks, and reference graphs. Tools such as Valgrind's `memcheck` or AddressSanitizer detect leaks and invalid accesses by instrumenting memory operations in native code:

```
valgrind --leak-check=full ./my_native_app
```

Output includes summary statistics:

```
==12345== LEAK SUMMARY:
==12345==    definitely lost: 1024 bytes in 10 blocks
==12345==    indirectly lost: 0 bytes in 0 blocks
==12345==      possibly lost: 512 bytes in 5 blocks
==12345==    still reachable: 2048 bytes in 20 blocks
```

Managed code profilers like VisualVM and dotMemory enable heap dump comparisons over time. By inspecting retained object sets and class instances, developers can isolate growing memory footprints. Aggregating allocation call stacks reveals what code paths are responsible for suspect objects.

Detecting and Analyzing Race Conditions

Race conditions arise from concurrent execution contexts accessing shared resources without proper synchronization, causing non-deterministic behavior, data corruption, or deadlock. Their detection requires capturing concurrent events and analyzing memory accesses and synchronization operations.

Dynamic data race detectors augment the program with instrumentation that monitors thread memory operations, exposing unsynchronized conflicting accesses. Tools such as ThreadSanitizer (TSan) for C/C++ and Intel Inspector use this approach:

```
clang++ -fsanitize=thread -g -O1 -o myprogram myprogram.cpp
./myprogram
```

TSan outputs detailed reports on conflicting memory accesses, including stack traces of involved threads, lock states, and synchronization barriers. For managed runtimes, profilers integrate thread state views to track locking primitives and detect starvation or race-prone code patterns.

Static analysis complements dynamic detection by examining source or bytecode for unsafe concurrent patterns. While lacking runtime context, it can identify missing volatile declarations, unsynchronized fields, or improper use of atomic operations. Combining static and dynamic methods yields more comprehensive detection.

Profiling Methodologies for Managed and Native Code

Profiling managed code necessitates awareness of runtime-specific factors such as Just-In-Time (JIT) compilation, garbage collection pauses, and thread scheduling policies. Events like JIT compilation introduce transient delays representative in profiling data but distinct from application logic inefficiencies. High-resolution profilers integrate runtime event streams with CPU metrics to disambiguate overhead sources.

In .NET environments, the Event Tracing for Windows (ETW) framework allows capturing detailed performance events while maintaining low overhead, facilitating precise temporal correlation of garbage collection, thread pool activities, and application code execution. Similarly, Java Flight Recorder (JFR) leverages low-impact event streaming to profile production workloads continuously.

Native-code profiling is more straightforward regarding runtime introspection but must consider variability in CPU architectures, cache hierarchies, and memory latency. Performance counters provide hardware-level insights, allowing identification of pipeline stalls and resource contentions that software profilers alone cannot elucidate.

Cross-layer profilers such as Intel VTune amplify this capability by combining hardware event data with source-level debugging symbols, enabling root-cause analysis from assembly instructions back to source lines.

Best Practices in Profiling and Analysis

Effective profiling involves balancing overhead, collection duration, and environmental fidelity. Sampling profilers should be employed first to gather broad insights with minimal perturbation. Following identification of suspect hot paths or suspicious allocations, focused instrumentation provides precise measurements to guide optimization.

Repeated profiling across different workloads and configurations ensures robustness of findings. Profiling production environments with lightweight tools such as eBPF-based tracers can reveal performance issues not apparent under test conditions.

Finally, profiling results must be interpreted considering domain-specific logic and algorithmic characteristics. Optimization without context can yield minimal gains or introduce regressions, underscoring the need for expert analysis integrated with profiling data.

Profiling tools and performance analysis form the foundation of informed optimization workflows, enabling precise improvements in speed, memory usage, and concurrency behavior for both managed and native codebases.

7.5. Static and Dynamic Code Analysis

Modern software development demands rigorous code quality assurance to maintain reliability, maintainability, and security. For Delphi applications, this necessitates leveraging sophisticated tools that perform both static and dynamic analysis, enabling developers to detect issues early and uphold coding standards automatically.

Static code analysis inspects source code without executing it, identifying potential errors, suspicious constructs, or deviations from coding guidelines. Popular tools for Delphi include **Pascal Analyzer (PAL)**, **Peganza**, and **FixInsight**, which parse Delphi's Object Pascal code to provide granular insights.

Static Analysis Techniques: Static analyzers parse source files to generate abstract syntax trees (AST) or intermediate representations, enabling comprehensive rule checks. These rules encompass syntax correctness, type safety, pointer usage, memory allocation patterns, and conformance to architectural patterns. Tools often classify issues into categories such as

- Syntax and semantic errors: Undeclared variables, incompatible assignments, or incorrect function calls.

- Code smells and anti-patterns: Methods with excessive complexity, unused variables, or duplicate code blocks.

- Security vulnerabilities: Buffer overflows, SQL injection risks via unsafe string handling, or improper exception management.

- Resource leaks: Unreleased handles, unfreed objects, or improper use of pointers leading to memory corruption.

For example, FixInsight integrates with the Delphi IDE and operates during compilation or on-demand, outputting warnings and errors directly in the output window. Its checks range from null pointer dereferences to violations of Object Pascal best practices.

```
procedure ProcessData(Data: Pointer);
begin
  // Potential null pointer dereference detected
  if Data^.Value > 0 then
    Process(Data);
end;
```

Static analysis tools often include linting capabilities, enforcing adherence to coding standards. This involves enforcing naming conventions, consistent indentation, preferring explicit type declarations, and prohibiting deprecated language features. Automating such checks drastically reduces manual code review overhead and ensures team-wide uniformity.

Dynamic Code Analysis complements static methods by executing the program and monitoring runtime behavior. Dynamic tools focus on detecting bugs that only manifest under certain runtime conditions, such as memory corruption, race conditions, or logic errors.

Tools like MADExcept and EurekaLog extend Delphi applications with exception monitoring and memory diagnostics, capturing call stacks and contextual information when an error occurs. Similarly, integrated dynamic analysis frameworks introduce instrumentation to detect heap corruption or invalid pointer use by monitoring memory allocations.

Example of Dynamic Bug Detection: Consider a scenario where an application corrupts the heap only when processing specific input data. Static analysis might not uncover this elusive bug if the code syntax and logic appear correct. Dynamic analysis tools instrument relevant code paths and track memory operations during execution.

```
Exception: Access Violation
Call Stack:
TMyClass.DoProcess
TMyClass.HandleInput
...
Memory block corrupted at 0x007FFB12
```

By automatically capturing such data at runtime, developers can pinpoint and resolve issues that traditional debugging may overlook.

Integrating static and dynamic analysis into continuous integration pipelines further streamlines quality assurance. Automated analysis runs upon each commit, providing immediate feedback on code health and preventing regressions. Combining this with code coverage measurement tools facilitates precise assessment of test adequacy and encourages robust test suites.

A generalized workflow for incorporating these tools in a Delphi project typically follows:

1. Execute static analysis (e.g., Pascal Analyzer) to identify syntax, style, and complexity issues.

2. Apply linting rules via integrated tools to enforce coding stan-

dards.

3. Run unit and integration tests instrumented with dynamic analyzers to detect runtime anomalies.

4. Capture and report exceptions and memory issues with tools like MADExcept or EurekaLog.

5. Iterate on findings, prioritize fixes, and re-run analyses to verify resolutions.

The benefits of automated static and dynamic code analysis include significant reduction in manual code audits, early defect detection, enhanced code readability, and sustained adherence to best practices. These improvements directly translate to increased software quality, reduced maintenance costs, and higher developer productivity.

Contemporary Delphi development environments increasingly embed or integrate these advanced analysis tools, offering developers comprehensive mechanisms to enforce quality at multiple stages of the development lifecycle. This holistic approach is essential for producing robust, secure, and performant software in complex enterprise environments.

7.6. Continuous Integration and Delivery

Continuous Integration and Delivery (CI/CD) represent cornerstone methodologies for modern software development, enabling rapid, reliable, and repeatable delivery of software artifacts. These practices automate the process of building, testing, and deployment, bridging the gap between development and operations. The implementation of CI/CD pipelines is instrumental in accelerating development velocity while simultaneously reinforcing software confidence through early and continuous validation.

At the heart of CI is the automation of the build and testing process. Developers frequently integrate their code changes into a shared repository, triggering a pipeline that compiles the application and executes an extensive suite of automated tests. This frequent and incremental integration addresses the problem of "integration hell" by uncovering defects and inconsistencies early. A typical CI pipeline includes the following core stages:

- Source code retrieval,

- Dependency resolution,

- Compilation or build,

- Unit and integration testing,

- Static code analysis.

Continuous Delivery builds upon CI by automating the deployment of validated builds to staging or production-like environments, ensuring that software is always in a releasable state. This automated deployment process allows teams to release new features and fixes faster while mitigating risks inherent in manual release processes. Continuous Deployment, a further extension, automatically releases every change that passes the CI pipeline to production, allowing for immediate feedback and rapid iteration.

The design of CI/CD pipelines requires careful orchestration of tools, scripts, and infrastructure. Popular CI/CD platforms such as Jenkins, GitLab CI/CD, CircleCI, and GitHub Actions provide the framework for defining pipelines as code. This infrastructure-as-code approach ensures that pipelines themselves are version-controlled and reproducible. Below is an illustrative example of a declarative CI/CD pipeline configuration segment, typical in Jenkins Pipeline syntax:

```
pipeline {
    agent any
    stages {
```

```
        stage('Checkout') {
            steps {
                checkout scm
            }
        }
        stage('Build') {
            steps {
                sh './gradlew clean build'
            }
        }
        stage('Test') {
            steps {
                sh './gradlew test'
                junit '**/build/test-results/test/*.xml'
            }
        }
        stage('Deploy') {
            when {
                branch 'main'
            }
            steps {
                sh './scripts/deploy.sh'
            }
        }
    }
    post {
        always {
            archiveArtifacts artifacts: '**/build/libs/*.jar',
    fingerprint: true
            cleanWs()
        }
        failure {
            mail to: 'dev-team@example.com',
                subject: "Build Failed: ${env.JOB_NAME}",
                body: "Build ${env.BUILD_NUMBER} failed. Check
    console output for details."
        }
    }
}
```

This pipeline illustrates key principles: separation of concerns across stages, conditional deployment only from the main branch, artifact archiving for traceability, and failure notification. Implementing such pipelines ensures immediate feedback loops for developers and maintains artifact integrity across environments.

Best practices for integrating CI/CD workflows encompass both technical and organizational dimensions. First, the pipeline should be as fast and deterministic as possible to enable quick feedback; this may require parallelizing test execution and caching dependencies. Second, pipelines must be resilient, incorporating retry logic and clear reporting mechanisms. Third, managing secrets and credentials securely, often via vaults or encrypted storage, prevents security breaches. Fourth, pipelines should produce immutable artifacts tagged with unique identifiers to guarantee traceability and reproducibility across environments.

Version control integration extends beyond source code to encompass infrastructure, configurations, and even pipeline definitions, reinforcing the concept of immutable infrastructure and configuration drift prevention. Comprehensive test coverage, including unit, integration, performance, and security tests, is imperative in reducing the risk of regressions and vulnerabilities. Automated rollback and canary deployment strategies further enhance confidence in production releases by enabling safe, incremental launches and rapid recovery.

The CI/CD pipelines also benefit from continuous monitoring and metrics collection. Tracking pipeline duration, failure rates, and deployment frequencies yields data essential for process optimization. Additionally, pipeline logs and audit trails facilitate troubleshooting and compliance with regulatory requirements.

Successful implementation of CI/CD pipelines transforms software delivery into a high-velocity, low-risk process. By automating builds, tests, and deployments and adhering to best practices, development teams gain not only acceleration but also enhanced confidence in software quality. This integration of workflows is indispensable for organizations aiming to innovate rapidly while maintaining operational excellence.

Chapter 8

Cross-Platform, Mobile, and Cloud Integration

Break free from platform boundaries and tap into the cloud-powered future with Delphi's unified development ecosystem. This chapter guides you through the essential patterns, APIs, and best practices for delivering seamless applications across desktop, mobile, and cloud environments—enabling your software to reach users wherever they are, on any device.

8.1. Building Multi-Platform Applications

Developing applications that run seamlessly across multiple platforms such as Windows, macOS, iOS, Android, and Linux requires addressing distinct differences in operating systems, user interface paradigms, hardware capabilities, and runtime environments. The FireMonkey (FMX) framework in Delphi provides an integrated solution designed to abstract platform-specific details while enabling developers to maintain a single codebase. Combining FMX with conditional compilation and platform abstractions allows the creation of high-performance, native applications tailored to each target operating system without fragmenting development efforts.

FireMonkey is a cross-platform GUI framework built atop GPU-accelerated vector graphics, offering rich visual components and a consistent application lifecycle across supported platforms. FMX components adapt dynamically to the conventions and user experience patterns expected on each platform, such as native-style controls on macOS or touch-friendly interfaces on mobile devices.

The core philosophy of FMX revolves around a unified component set that includes controls, layouts, and animations. Developers interact with FMX's component hierarchy and event model identically regardless of the deployment target, benefiting from underlying implementations optimized per platform. Graphics abstraction layers handle disparate drawing APIs, for example, Direct2D on Windows, Metal on macOS and iOS, and OpenGL or Vulkan variants on Android and Linux.

Key benefits of FMX include:

- **Unified Styling and Theming**: Through the TStyleBook component, visual consistency can be maintained or customized per platform.

- **Cross-Platform Components**: Controls such as TButton, TListBox, and TMemo adapt behavior and rendering to conform with platform standards.

- **Hardware Acceleration**: Leveraging GPU acceleration ensures responsiveness and efficient animations across devices.

However, achieving optimal user experience often requires fine-tuning beyond FMX's default behavior, necessitating platform-specific interventions within the common codebase.

Conditional compilation directives ($IFDEF, $IFNDEF) enable selective inclusion of code according to the target platform at compile time, preserving a single codebase while addressing divergence in APIs or platform norms. Delphi provides predefined compiler symbols for major platforms:

- MSWINDOWS for Windows

- MACOS for macOS

- IOS for iOS

- ANDROID for Android

- LINUX for Linux (primarily Linux 64-bit)

These symbols can be combined or nested to differentiate functionality. For example, a file path access routine may differ between desktop and mobile platforms, or hardware-specific APIs can be conditionally invoked only when certain capabilities exist.

```
function GetConfigPath: string;
begin
  {$IF DEFINED(MSWINDOWS)}
  Result := System.IOUtils.TPath.Combine(System.IOUtils.TPath.
    GetHomePath, 'App\Config');
  {$ELSEIF DEFINED(MACOS)}
  Result := System.IOUtils.TPath.Combine(System.IOUtils.TPath.
    GetLibraryPath, 'Application Support/App/Config');
  {$ELSEIF DEFINED(IOS) OR DEFINED(ANDROID)}
  Result := System.IOUtils.TPath.Combine(System.IOUtils.TPath.
    GetDocumentsPath, 'Config');
  {$ELSE}
  Result := '/etc/app/config';
  {$ENDIF}
end;
```

Using conditional compilation judiciously confines platform-specific complexities to targeted blocks, improving code readability and maintainability.

187

Beyond UI differences, many applications require platform-dependent services such as file system access, network communication, notifications, sensors, or hardware peripherals. Building abstraction layers encapsulates these variations behind common interfaces, allowing higher-level logic to remain platform-agnostic.

A recommended approach is to define interfaces representing platform-dependent functionalities and implement these interfaces in separate units or classes per platform, selected via conditional compilation. The Factory design pattern is often employed to instantiate platform-specific implementations transparently at runtime or compile time.

For example, consider accessing a device's GPS location:

```
type
  ILocationService = interface
    ['{9A7D8E5B-224C-4B9F-B35A-12C8C8D99C8D}']
    procedure StartTracking;
    procedure StopTracking;
    function GetCurrentLocation: TPointF;
  end;

{$IF DEFINED(ANDROID)}
uses
  AndroidApi.Location;

type
  TAndroidLocationService = class(TInterfacedObject,
    ILocationService)
  public
    procedure StartTracking;
    procedure StopTracking;
    function GetCurrentLocation: TPointF;
  end;
{$ENDIF}

{$IF DEFINED(IOS)}
uses
  iOSapi.CoreLocation;

type
  TIOSLocationService = class(TInterfacedObject, ILocationService
    )
  public
    procedure StartTracking;
```

188

```
    procedure StopTracking;
    function GetCurrentLocation: TPointF;
  end;
{$ENDIF}
```

A factory function returns the correct implementation based on the current platform:

```
function CreateLocationService: ILocationService;
begin
  {$IF DEFINED(ANDROID)}
  Result := TAndroidLocationService.Create;
  {$ELSEIF DEFINED(IOS)}
  Result := TIOSLocationService.Create;
  {$ELSE}
  Result := nil; // Unsupported platform or default
    implementation
  {$ENDIF}
end;
```

Such encapsulation promotes clean separation of concerns, enabling easier testing, extension, and debugging.

User interaction models vary markedly across desktop and mobile environments, affecting keyboard usage, touch gestures, mouse input, and accessibility requirements. FMX provides abstracted event handlers such as OnClick, OnGesture, and OnKeyUp that unify input management, yet developers must consider platform conventions to optimize usability.

For instance, right-click context menus are common on desktop OSes but absent on mobile platforms where long-press or swipe gestures provide analogous functionality. A conditional approach simplifies distinction:

```
procedure TForm1.ControlMouseUp(Sender: TObject; Button:
    TMouseButton; Shift: TShiftState; X, Y: Single);
begin
  {$IF DEFINED(MSWINDOWS) OR DEFINED(MACOS)}
  if Button = TMouseButton.mbRight then
    PopupContextMenu.PopupAt(CursorPos);
  {$ENDIF}
end;

procedure TForm1.ControlGesture(Sender: TObject; const EventInfo:
    TGestureEventInfo; var Handled: Boolean);
```

```
begin
  {$IF DEFINED(IOS) OR DEFINED(ANDROID)}
  if EventInfo.GestureID = sgiLongTap then
  begin
    PopupContextMenu.PopupAt(PointF(EventInfo.Location.X,
     EventInfo.Location.Y));
    Handled := True;
  end;
  {$ENDIF}
end;
```

UI layouts benefit from FMX's flexible layout controls and device metrics awareness. The TDeviceInfo class provides platform and device-specific properties used to conditionally adapt scaling, font sizes, and control arrangements to accommodate screen resolutions and DPI differences.

Delphi's multi-platform compiler toolchain facilitates cross-compilation, enabling a developer to build binaries for Windows, macOS, iOS, Android, and Linux from a single IDE instance. Platform-specific SDKs and toolchains (e.g., Xcode for iOS/macOS, Android SDK for Android) must be installed and configured correctly for the IDE to perform compilation and deployment operations.

Key steps include:

- Installing and linking platform SDKs and signing certificates for mobile targets.

- Using Delphi's Platform Selector to switch target platforms.

- Managing platform-specific project options such as compiler defines, deployment paths, and permissions.

- Executing remote or local debugging sessions tailored to each platform's runtime environment.

Automated build scripts and continuous integration pipelines can leverage command-line tools such as msbuild combined with Delphi's platform-aware project files to orchestrate multi-platform app generation.

- Design UI and business logic layers with platform independence, leveraging FMX for visual abstraction.

- Use conditional compilation strategically to inject platform-specific code without cluttering the core logic.

- Encapsulate access to platform-dependent services behind interfaces and employ factory patterns to instantiate correct implementations.

- Adapt user input handling and UI behavior to respect platform conventions, ensuring an intuitive user experience.

- Maintain a flexible project structure with proper SDK integration to streamline build and deployment workflows.

- Continuously test on target platforms and devices to uncover subtle platform-specific issues early.

Mastering these techniques equips developers to build robust, maintainable Delphi applications capable of reaching broad user bases while minimizing duplicated effort and complexity inherent in multi-platform development.

8.2. Mobile Development for iOS and Android

Delphi offers a robust framework for native mobile development on both iOS and Android platforms through its FireMonkey (FMX) application framework. Exploiting native APIs, Delphi allows developers to access device-specific features such as sensors, notifications, and local storage, while maintaining high performance and a near-native user experience. This section details the essential components and best practices for interfacing with these device functionalities, alongside preparing applications for deployment and ensuring compliance with app store guidelines.

Mobile applications often rely on sensor data to deliver contextual and interactive experiences. Delphi's Mobile APIs provide abstractions over device sensors, enabling easy integration with accelerometers, gyroscopes, magnetometers, GPS units, and ambient light sensors. The TCustomSensor component hierarchy within the System.Sensors unit serves as a primary interface.

For instance, accessing accelerometer data involves creating and configuring a TAccelerometerSensor instance. One must initialize the sensor, set the desired update interval, and implement the OnNotify event handler to process sensor data asynchronously. This event delivers a TData record with individual axis measurements.

```
uses
   System.Sensors, System.Sensors.Components;

var
   Accelerometer: TCustomAccelerometer;

procedure SetupAccelerometer;
begin
   Accelerometer := TSensorManager.Current.GetSensorsByCategory(
      TSensorCategory.Motion).FindSensor(TSensorType.Accelerometer
      );
   if Assigned(Accelerometer) then
   begin
      Accelerometer.OnNotify := AccelerometerNotify;
      Accelerometer.Accuracy := TSensorAccuracy.High;
      Accelerometer.Active := True;
   end;
end;

procedure AccelerometerNotify(Sender: TObject; const AData:
      TSensorData; const AReadingTime: TDateTime);
begin
   // Process accelerometer data
   // e.g., AData.Acceleration.X, AData.Acceleration.Y, AData.
      Acceleration.Z
end;
```

It is critical to manage sensor activation judiciously to conserve battery life, enabling sensors only when necessary and disabling them promptly after use.

Notifications are vital in maintaining user engagement through timely alerts. Delphi supports both local and push notifications, with platform-specific services abstracted into the FMX framework.

Local notifications can be scheduled via the TNotificationCenter component. A notification is constructed with properties specifying its title, message, badge number, and trigger time. Notification channels (particularly on Android Oreo and later) must be configured to categorize notification behaviors such as importance, sound, and vibration.

The following code snippet illustrates scheduling a simple local notification:

```
uses
   System.Notification;

var
  NotificationCenter: TNotificationCenter;
  Notification: TNotification;

procedure ScheduleNotification;
begin
  NotificationCenter := TNotificationCenter.Create(nil);
  if NotificationCenter.Supported then
  begin
    Notification := NotificationCenter.CreateNotification;
    Notification.AlertBody := 'This is a local notification';
    Notification.Title := 'Delphi FMX Notification';
    Notification.FireTime := Now + EncodeTime(0,1,0,0); // 1
    minute later
    NotificationCenter.ScheduleNotification(Notification);
  end;
end;
```

For push notifications, integration with Firebase Cloud Messaging (for Android) and Apple Push Notification Service (APNs) requires additional platform-specific configuration, including certificates and provisioning profiles, outside the scope of Delphi's direct APIs but accessible through native helper libraries and platform services.

Mobile apps demand reliable local storage mechanisms for caching, offline operation, and user preferences. Delphi offers multiple approaches, encompassing:

- **File-based storage**: Using TFileStream, TMemoryStream, or direct TFile operations to read/write files in sandboxed app directories.

- **SQLite databases**: Through FireDAC or third-party components, embedding SQLite enables structured data persistence with SQL querying capabilities.

- **Platform-specific storage APIs**: Accessing shared preferences on Android or NSUserDefaults on iOS via platform services or Objective-C bridging.

A common pattern for persistent settings is to employ TIniFile or TMemIniFile analogs adapted for mobile, writing configuration data within application documents directory. For example, retrieving the documents path ensures compliance with sandboxing rules:

```
uses
  System.IOUtils;

var
  AppDocumentsPath: string;

begin
  AppDocumentsPath := TPath.GetDocumentsPath;
  // Use AppDocumentsPath to save or load user data files
end;
```

SQLite databases are typically located within the same documents directory, facilitating backups and data migration in line with platform expectations.

The final stages of mobile app development include configuring deployment settings, signing, and adhering to platform policies and guidelines to ensure smooth submission to Google Play Store and Apple App Store.

Delphi's Project Manager allows specifying target platforms, architectures (ARM64 being mandatory for latest devices), and build configurations. Key considerations include:

- **Code Signing and Provisioning**: iOS applications require provisioning profiles and certificates provided by Apple's Developer Portal. Android builds use `keystore` files for signing. Delphi integrates these through the Platform SDK manager and Deployment options.

- **App Icons and Launch Screens**: Both platforms mandate inclusion of multiple resolution assets. Delphi's resource manager facilitates embedding these, but developers must prepare platform-compliant images manually.

- **Permission Declarations**: Access to sensors, storage, or notifications necessitates declaring permissions in `AndroidManifest.xml` or iOS `Info.plist`. Delphi provides editor support for these manifests when deploying.

- **64-bit and API Level Compliance**: Google Play mandates 64-bit support and targeting recent API levels. Similarly, Apple requires adherence to the latest SDKs and hardware capabilities.

Comprehensive testing on physical devices and emulators is essential to validate behavior across hardware variations and OS versions. Delphi's Live Preview and remote debugging capabilities accelerate this process.

Beyond technical constraints, apps must satisfy a range of guidelines imposed by Apple and Google, predominantly concerning privacy, security, and user experience. Specific steps include:

- **Privacy Policy Integration**: Applications accessing personal data or sensors must present clear privacy disclosures. Developers should embed privacy URLs or text within app submissions and respect user permissions.

- **Secure Data Handling**: Sensitive information stored locally or transmitted externally should be encrypted. While Delphi does not mandate encryption methods, developers can leverage the System.Hash and cryptographic libraries for such safeguards.

- **User Consent Dialogs**: On iOS particularly, use of sensors like cameras or location demands runtime user permissions. Delphi includes APIs to trigger permission requests and process user responses.

- **Adherence to UI Guidelines**: Both platforms emphasize intuitive navigation and accessible design. Although FMX supports cross-platform UI components, tailoring layouts for each device family is often necessary.

Automating parts of the deployment pipeline through continuous integration and delivery tools can assist in maintaining consistency and compliance, reducing iteration times when preparing app updates or new releases.

Delphi's native mobile development stack empowers developers to fully leverage the capabilities of iOS and Android devices. By mastering sensor integration, notifications, local storage, and rigorous deployment procedures, software engineers can produce performant, compliant, and user-centric mobile applications.

8.3. Interfacing with Native Libraries and APIs

Delphi's capability to interface with native libraries and external APIs is a cornerstone for harnessing platform-specific functionality and extending application reach beyond the managed runtime. This interfacing leverages Foreign Function Interfaces (FFI), enabling seamless interaction with code libraries written in C, C++, and system-level APIs provided by Windows, macOS, Linux, and mobile platforms. Mastery of FFI, marshaling techniques, and binding conventions is essential for ensuring robust, performant, and maintainable integrations.

At the heart of Delphi's foreign interfacing is the `external` directive, which declares functions and procedures implemented outside the Delphi unit, typically residing in dynamic-link libraries (DLLs) or shared libraries (`.so`, `.dylib`). A minimal external function declaration appears as follows:

```
function MessageBox(hWnd: HWND; lpText, lpCaption: PChar; uType:
    UINT): Integer; stdcall; external 'user32.dll';
```

Here, `stdcall` defines the calling convention, crucial for calling compatibility and stack cleanup; mismatched conventions often lead to runtime faults or stack corruption. The declaration explicitly identifies the DLL containing the procedure, enabling the Delphi linker and runtime loader to locate and bind the symbol correctly.

Marshaling is the process of converting data types and memory layouts between Delphi and foreign environments. Careful marshaling ensures that parameters passed by value or reference remain consistent in semantics and representation. Consider the mapping of Delphi `string` types to C-style null-terminated `char*` pointers: Delphi's `AnsiString`, `WideString`, and `UnicodeString` differ in encoding and memory management, requiring explicit conversion or usage of pointer types like `PAnsiChar` or `PWideChar`. For instance:

```
var
  Msg, Caption: string;
begin
  Msg := 'Hello, World';
  Caption := 'Delphi MessageBox';
  MessageBox(0, PChar(Msg), PChar(Caption), MB_OK);
end;
```

This code performs implicit conversion from string to PChar compatible with the Windows API. For more precise control, explicit conversion routines such as SysUtils.StrPCopy or UTF8Encode can be employed, especially when interfacing with UTF-8 encoded libraries.

Complex data structures and callbacks present additional challenges in marshaling. Structures shared between Delphi and C require identical memory layouts, typically enforced using the packed record and {align*} compiler directives to suppress compiler-introduced padding and align fields as per the target ABI. For example:

```
type
  TPoint = packed record
    X: Integer;
    Y: Integer;
  end;
```

If the native library exposes function pointers for callbacks, Delphi methods need to be adapted to match the signature strictly by declaring compatible procedural types with the correct calling conventions and parameters. For instance:

```
type
  TCallback = procedure(Value: Integer); cdecl;

procedure RegisterCallback(cb: TCallback); cdecl; external '
    native.dll';
```

The use of cdecl or stdcall depends on the foreign API's calling convention, and failure to match these can lead to stack corruption.

Binding third-party libraries often involves more than simple function imports; sometimes headers in C must be translated manually or with automated tools such as Pascal header converters. For extensive APIs, detailed Pascal interface units are developed to provide type-safe access. Consider the example of binding to a native JSON parsing library:

```
type
  PJSONObject = Pointer;

function json_parse(json: PAnsiChar): PJSONObject; cdecl;
    external 'libjson.so';

procedure json_free(obj: PJSONObject); cdecl; external 'libjson.
    so';
```

Memory ownership and lifecycle management become critical here; the Delphi side must respect the allocation and deallocation semantics defined by the native library to avoid leaks or invalid memory access.

Delphi also allows dynamic binding using LoadLibrary and GetProcAddress for loading shared libraries at runtime. This approach is vital for optional features or plugin architectures. Sample usage:

```
var
  LibHandle: THandle;
  FuncPtr: function(A: Integer): Integer; cdecl;
begin
  LibHandle := LoadLibrary('mylib.dll');
  if LibHandle <> 0 then
  begin
    @FuncPtr := GetProcAddress(LibHandle, 'FunctionName');
    if Assigned(FuncPtr) then
      WriteLn(FuncPtr(42));
    FreeLibrary(LibHandle);
  end;
end;
```

Such dynamic interfacing demands meticulous error checking and resource management but offers flexibility in modular application design.

Platform-specific native APIs, such as Win32, macOS Cocoa, or Android NDK libraries, expose rich functionality inaccessible through cross-platform RTL units. Delphi's ability to interface with these via FFIs extends applications with native UI elements, hardware access, or optimizations. For example, accessing Windows Registry functions or macOS native notifications integrates deeply with the OS environment.

Integration with native graphical APIs (DirectX, OpenGL, Metal) or hardware interfaces (Bluetooth, sensors) necessitates precise marshaling of memory buffers and synchronization primitives. In such scenarios, passing pointers to untyped memory and ensuring thread safety requires careful design and sometimes platform-specific wrappers.

Delphi's foreign function interfaces underpin powerful interoperability, enabling developers to harness system-level features and third-party native libraries while preserving type safety and runtime stability. Key considerations include adherence to calling conventions, rigorous marshaling of data types, compatibility of data structures, and correct lifecycles of dynamically allocated resources. Mastery of these concepts unlocks the full potential of Delphi as a systems programming language with rich cross-platform and native capabilities.

8.4. Cloud Services Integration

Connecting modern applications to leading cloud services through RESTful APIs requires a comprehensive approach to authentication, data management, and service orchestration. This integration enables applications to leverage scalable cloud storage, messaging systems, and serverless functions, facilitating significant modernization and scalability.

REST (Representational State Transfer) APIs serve as the primary communication interface with cloud services. Each resource in the cloud service is accessed via HTTP methods—GET, POST, PUT, DELETE—using URIs that represent object endpoints. JSON is conventionally the preferred payload format due to its efficiency and readability.

Cloud providers expose RESTful APIs that encapsulate their service capabilities, such as object storage, identity management, event triggering, and messaging. Integration necessitates accurate construction of HTTP requests with proper headers, query parameters, and body content conforming to each service's specification.

Authentication is fundamental when invoking cloud REST APIs. Most leading providers employ OAuth 2.0, API keys, or token-based mechanisms to secure access. Understanding and implementing these authentication methods correctly is vital for both security and functional integration.

OAuth 2.0 provides delegated access using access tokens obtained from authorization servers. The typical flow involves:

- Obtaining client credentials (client ID and client secret).
- Redirecting users or applications to an authorization endpoint to grant permission.
- Exchanging authorization codes or credentials for an access token.
- Attaching the access token in the HTTP `Authorization` header for subsequent requests as a Bearer token.

Tokens typically expire and require refreshing using refresh tokens to maintain session continuity without repeated user interaction.

Some services support API keys passed in headers or query strings. More sensitive operations may require cryptographic signature generation (e.g., AWS Signature Version 4), which involves creating a canonical request, hashing, and signing using secret keys to ensure message authenticity and integrity.

```
import requests

access_token = "YOUR_ACCESS_TOKEN"
headers = {
    "Authorization": f"Bearer {access_token}",
    "Content-Type": "application/json"
}
response = requests.get("https://api.cloudprovider.com/v1/
    resources", headers=headers)
```

Cloud storage APIs typically expose capabilities for managing buckets and objects (files). Operations include upload, download, listing, and deletion of objects, as well as metadata manipulation.

For optimal performance and consistency:

- Utilize multipart upload APIs for large objects to improve transfer reliability.

- Implement exponential backoff and retry strategies to handle transient errors or throttling.

- Leverage signed URLs to grant temporary access without exposing credentials.

Example RESTful interactions involve:

- PUT requests to upload files or update metadata.

- GET requests to retrieve or list objects.

- DELETE requests to remove objects or buckets.

Cloud messaging services provide decoupled communication via queues and topics, supporting asynchronous processing and event-driven architectures.

Key integration tasks include:

- Publishing messages to a queue or topic through API calls.

- Subscribing and consuming messages with proper acknowledgment and visibility timeout management.

- Configuring filtering and routing rules where supported (e.g., message attributes).

Typical message payloads are JSON-encoded. Endpoints often require authentication tokens and may impose rate limits or quota restrictions handled by careful client design.

Serverless functions enable execution of code snippets triggered by HTTP events, cloud storage changes, messaging events, or scheduled timers. Integrating serverless functions offers elastic scaling, reduced operational overhead, and fine-grained billing.

Integration involves:

- Deploying function code using provider-specific tooling or APIs.

- Configuring triggers that invoke functions based on events from storage, messaging, or HTTP endpoints.

- Managing environment variables, execution roles, and timeout parameters for security and performance optimization.

- Capturing logs and monitoring invocation metrics via API endpoints or dashboards.

Invoking serverless functions directly via RESTful HTTP requests allows applications to incorporate complex processing and business logic without dedicated server infrastructure.

Effective cloud service integration requires architectural decisions focused on resilience, security, and maintainability:

- Abstract REST API interactions in modular service layers or SDK wrappers to shield application logic from API changes.

- Securely store and manage credentials using secrets management services or environment variables.

- Monitor API usage and implement quota management to prevent service disruption.

- Employ idempotency keys where supported to safely retry API requests without duplication.

- Validate input and sanitize outputs to prevent injection attacks and maintain data integrity.

- Design for eventual consistency where cloud services are distributed and asynchronous.

Robust logging of API calls and error handling ensures faster diagnostics and recovery in production environments.

```
import requests

access_token = "YOUR_ACCESS_TOKEN"
file_path = "/path/to/file.txt"
upload_url = "https://storage.cloudprovider.com/v1/buckets/my-
    bucket/objects/file.txt"

headers = {
    "Authorization": f"Bearer {access_token}",
    "Content-Type": "application/octet-stream"
}

with open(file_path, 'rb') as f:
    data = f.read()

response = requests.put(upload_url, headers=headers, data=data)

if response.status_code == 200:
    print("File uploaded successfully.")
else:
    print(f"Upload failed: {response.status_code} {response.text
        }")
```

File uploaded successfully.

This example illustrates establishing secure authenticated communication and performing a basic file upload operation. Similar pat-

terns apply for more complex workflows involving metadata annotation, multipart upload, or integration with serverless functions
triggered post-upload.

Cloud services' RESTful APIs provide rich, flexible mechanisms for
extending application capabilities beyond traditional on-premises
systems. Mastery of these interfaces, combined with effective authentication handling and programmatic orchestration, forms the
foundation for scalable, resilient, and maintainable cloud-native
applications.

8.5. Packaging and Deployment Strategies

Modern software systems demand sophisticated packaging and
deployment strategies to facilitate seamless distribution, reliable
updates, and security across heterogeneous target environments.
Packages must encapsulate application resources, dependencies,
and configuration metadata with precision, while deployment
mechanisms must accommodate diverse platform constraints and
operational contexts. This section examines advanced techniques
encompassing application packaging, custom installer creation,
over-the-air (OTA) update methodologies, and deployment
approaches optimized for robustness and security.

Advanced Application Packaging

Effective packaging consolidates all application components-
binaries, libraries, assets, configuration files-into a coherent,
reproducible, and manageable unit. Containerization has
become a fundamental strategy, leveraging lightweight runtime
environments that encapsulate the entire application stack, thus
standardizing execution across systems. Technologies such as
Docker employ layered file systems to optimize image size and
caching.

Beyond containers, language-specific package managers (e.g., npm for JavaScript, pip for Python, Maven for Java) remain critical for dependency resolution and version control. Advanced packaging requires integration of dependency locking (e.g., `package-lock.json`, `poetry.lock`) to ensure deterministic builds. Build tools like Bazel and Buck enable hermetic builds, automating artifact generation while tightly controlling inputs and outputs for reproducibility.

Custom package formats designed for target platforms permit enhanced control over installation processes and integration. For example, Windows Installer (MSI) packages support detailed control over prerequisites, component registration, and rollback mechanisms. On Linux, RPM and DEB formats permit rich metadata specification, script execution during install and removal, and dependency resolution leveraging native package managers.

The packaging workflow also involves signing packages cryptographically to ensure integrity and provenance verification. Public key infrastructure (PKI)-based signatures prevent tampering, while integrating with trusted certificate authorities to validate identity.

Custom Installer Creation

Custom installers provide a tailored user experience and can embed sophisticated logic beyond simple file extraction. Frameworks such as WiX Toolset for Windows and InstallShield offer declarative XML-based configuration or script-driven customization for complex installation workflows. Custom actions enable pre-install validation, environment checks, selective component installation, and post-install configuration.

For multiplatform applications, cross-platform installer tools like InstallBuilder and InstallAnywhere automate the generation of native installers for Windows, macOS, and Linux from a single specification. These tools often incorporate features such as localization, silent installation modes, and integration with system package providers.

The creation of custom installers must balance complexity with maintainability. Incorporating rollback support is critical in case of partial failures, ensuring the system state reverts cleanly without residual inconsistencies. Furthermore, the installer should support unattended installation automation compatible with enterprise deployment systems such as Microsoft System Center Configuration Manager (SCCM) or Ansible.

Typical installer scripts are often written as declarative recipes or embedded in domain-specific languages provided by installer tools. For example, an MSI custom action written in C# might perform environment detection:

```
UINT __stdcall CheckOSVersion(MSIHANDLE hInstall)
{
    OSVERSIONINFOEX osvi = { sizeof(OSVERSIONINFOEX) };
    if (!GetVersionEx((OSVERSIONINFO*)&osvi)) {
        return ERROR_INSTALL_FAILURE;
    }
    if (osvi.dwMajorVersion < 10) {
        // Log error: Unsupported OS version
        MsiProcessMessage(hInstall, INSTALLMESSAGE_ERROR,
            TEXT("This application requires Windows 10 or higher
        ."));
        return ERROR_INSTALL_FAILURE;
    }
    return ERROR_SUCCESS;
}
```

Over-the-Air Update Mechanisms

OTA updates enable remote delivery of application patches, new features, or critical fixes without requiring physical access to the device or manual reinstallation. Implementing OTA requires a robust update client integrated into the application or operating system agent, capable of securely querying update servers, downloading incremental packages, and applying updates atomically.

A frequent strategy involves differential updates that transmit only changed segments to minimize bandwidth and reduce update time. Binary delta patching algorithms such as bsdiff or

Google's `Courgette` transform a base binary into the target version with minimal data transmitted. Combining this with content-addressable storage systems and versioned artifacts fosters efficiency and reliability.

Secure delivery is paramount. All update packages are signed, and the client must verify both the package signature and integrity using cryptographic hash functions before execution. To counter rollback attacks, update metadata should include monotonic version identifiers enforced by the client to reject older or revoked packages.

An OTA update cycle generally follows these steps:

- Query update manifest from secure server
- If a newer version is available:
  - Download update package (full or delta)
  - Verify package signature and hash
  - If verification succeeds:
    * Apply update atomically (e.g., swap binaries)
    * Restart or reload application components
  - Else:
    * Report failure and revert to prior state

Distributed update infrastructures employ Content Delivery Networks (CDNs) for scalability, edge caching to reduce latency, and authentication tokens to restrict access. Rollback mechanisms protect against faulty updates by preserving the last known good application state.

Reliable and Secure Deployment Models

Deployments must guarantee high availability, security, and consistency regardless of target platform and network conditions.

Strategies incorporate redundancy, failover, and atomic state transitions.

For enterprise-grade deployments, orchestration platforms like Kubernetes manage containerized application lifecycles, providing declarative deployment via manifests. Kubernetes concepts such as rolling updates and health probes enable zero-downtime deployment by incrementally replacing instances while continuously monitoring their state.

On embedded or constrained devices, dual-bank flash memory architecture permits an active partition for app execution and an inactive partition for staged updates-ensuring rollback on failure. Bootloaders verify image integrity and signatures before execution, preventing execution of corrupted or malicious code.

Security encompasses transport encryption (TLS) for download channels, mutual authentication between client and server, secure storage of cryptographic keys on devices (e.g., using hardware security modules), and sandboxed execution environments restricting update scope. Deployment automation must enforce least-privilege principles to minimize attack surfaces.

In hybrid environments spanning cloud, edge, and on-premises, deployment pipelines leverage continuous integration and continuous delivery (CI/CD) tools combined with infrastructure-as-code. Techniques such as blue-green deployments and canary releases mitigate risks by gradually diverting traffic to new versions, enabling monitoring and rapid rollback.

Integrating deployment telemetry-capturing success rates, failure modes, and performance metrics-supports adaptive decision-making for update policies and rollback thresholds. This closed feedback loop enhances robustness and promotes continuous improvement.

- Structure packages to ensure complete dependency encapsulation and reproducible builds.

- Employ cryptographic signing and verification to protect package integrity.

- Design custom installers that incorporate validation, rollback, and automation features suitable for the target platform.

- Implement OTA updates with secure, incremental delivery, atomic application of patches, and rollback mechanisms.

- Utilize deployment models that promote zero-downtime updates, secure execution, and integration with monitoring and orchestration tools.

The application of these strategies results in scalable, secure, and manageable software distribution capable of serving diverse environments and evolving operational requirements.

8.6. Monitoring and Telemetry

Effective monitoring and telemetry are indispensable for ensuring the reliability, performance, and maintainability of modern Delphi applications, especially those designed for cross-platform deployment and cloud environments. Implementing robust diagnostics, logging, remote monitoring, and analytics systems enables developers to detect issues early, understand user behavior comprehensively, and accelerate troubleshooting processes.

At the core of robust application monitoring lies systematic diagnostics capturing runtime information and error states. Delphi provides structured exception handling combined with detailed diagnostic capabilities through the Exception class hierarchy and extended RTTI (Run-Time Type Information). Leveraging these mechanisms, developers should instrument critical code paths to emit diagnostic events that include contextual information such as error codes, stack traces, and execution metrics. Employing conditional compilation directives ($IFDEF) allows the selective inclusion of diagnostic instrumentation for debug and release builds, minimizing performance overhead in production while retaining rich data during development and test cycles.

Logging strategies must be designed to balance verbosity, queryability, and minimal impact on application responsiveness. Cross-platform Delphi applications benefit from using a unified logging framework capable of targeting multiple backends, such as file systems, databases, or cloud logging services. The TLogger class or third-party libraries like Log4Delphi provide abstracted logging facilities with configurable log levels (Error, Warning, Info, Debug, Trace). Log entries should include timestamps, severity levels, categories, and optionally correlation identifiers to link related events within a distributed system. Integrating structured logging formats such as JSON enhances the parsing and filtering capabilities of log aggregation tools.

Remote monitoring amplifies the diagnostic process by allowing real-time visibility into running instances across heterogeneous environments. To implement remote monitoring, Delphi applications can be instrumented to emit telemetry data to centralized services via secure HTTP(s) APIs or messaging protocols (e.g., MQTT, AMQP). Leveraging cloud-native monitoring platforms such as Azure Monitor, AWS CloudWatch, or Prometheus assists in aggregating metrics, logs, and traces with minimal operational burden. Telemetry data generally encompasses application health metrics (CPU, memory usage, thread counts), business metrics (transaction rates, user sessions), and custom application-specific events indicative of business logic outcomes or feature usage. Implementing an asynchronous, non-blocking telemetry client ensures minimal interference with the application's primary workflows.

Analytics integration is crucial for transforming raw telemetry and log data into actionable insights. By correlating application performance data with user interaction metrics, developers gain fine-grained understanding of user behavior patterns and system bottlenecks. For cloud-enabled Delphi applications, feeding telemetry into analytics engines such as Azure Application Insights, Google Cloud Operations suite, or Elastic Stack allows querying via rich DSLs and visualization through dashboards. Custom instrumentation should focus on key performance indicators (KPIs) including application startup time, API latency distributions, error frequency, and session durations. Analyzing trends over time supports predictive maintenance and resource allocation optimization.

To facilitate rapid troubleshooting, error reporting must be designed for effective incident management. Delphi applications should automatically capture exceptions and system faults, enrich them with contextual diagnostics, and forward them to incident tracking platforms such as Sentry or Raygun. Instrumentation can include minimizing user disruption by capturing silent failures or providing friendly error feedback. Attaching user-specific metadata and environment descriptions (OS version, hardware info, network conditions) expedites root cause analysis. Incorporating unique correlation identifiers between logs, telemetry traces, and errors bridges observations across services and components in distributed architectures.

Cross-platform considerations impose additional challenges in monitoring infrastructure. Variations in filesystem structures, network stacks, and execution contexts demand adaptable telemetry clients. Utilizing platform-agnostic APIs for networking and storage combined with conditional platform-specific implementation ensures consistent telemetry behavior on Win32, macOS, Linux, iOS, and Android targets. Security is paramount-telemetry data must be transmitted over encrypted channels with authentication to prevent tampering or data leakage. Employing token-based authorization and adhering to privacy regulations (GDPR, CCPA) ensures compliance in user data handling.

Monitoring extensibility via plugin models or hooks inside the Delphi runtime enables integrating custom diagnostics tailored to application domain requirements. For instance, embedding detailed performance counters, memory profiling snapshots, or even user interface interaction traces enriches telemetry repositories. Coupled with continuous integration and deployment pipelines, automated monitoring health checks and regression alerts accelerate delivery cadence without compromising stability.

```
type
  TTelemetryClient = class
  private
    FHttpClient: THttpClient;
  public
    constructor Create;
    procedure LogEvent(const ACategory, AMessage: string; ALevel:
      Integer);
  end;

constructor TTelemetryClient.Create;
begin
  FHttpClient := THttpClient.Create;
  // Configure client with base URL and headers for telemetry
    endpoint
end;

procedure TTelemetryClient.LogEvent(const ACategory, AMessage:
    string; ALevel: Integer);
var
  Payload: TStringStream;
  JsonPayload: string;
begin
  JsonPayload := Format(
    '{"category": "%s", "message": "%s", "level": %d, "timestamp
      ": "%s"}',
    [ACategory, AMessage, ALevel, FormatDateTime('yyyy-mm-dd"T"hh
      :nn:ss"Z"', Now.UTC)]);
  Payload := TStringStream.Create(JsonPayload, TEncoding.UTF8);
  try
    // Post asynchronously without blocking main thread
    TTask.Run(procedure
    begin
      try
        FHttpClient.Post('https://telemetry.endpoint/api/logs',
      Payload);
```

```
      except
        // Handle transient failures (e.g., retry or buffer)
      end;
    end);
  finally
    Payload.Free;
  end;
end;
```

Example telemetry JSON payload:
```
{
  "category": "Performance",
  "message": "API response time exceeded threshold: 350ms",
  "level": 2,
  "timestamp": "2024-05-26T14:37:22Z"
}
```

Integration of monitoring and telemetry with Delphi's native event loops and multi-threading capabilities ensures minimal disruption of application responsiveness. Developers should adopt best practices such as batching telemetry transmissions, backpressure management, and fallback caching for offline scenarios.

The convergence of diagnostics, logging, remote monitoring, and analytics empowers Delphi applications to achieve high stability, deep operational insight, and swift troubleshooting across diverse platforms and cloud environments. Building such a comprehensive monitoring stack facilitates proactive maintenance, delivers superior user experience, and provides essential visibility for continuous improvement.

Chapter 9

Secure, Maintainable, and Sustainable Delphi Code

Long-lasting, resilient applications demand more than just clever algorithms—security, maintainability, and sustainability are their true hallmarks. In this chapter, discover best practices and advanced strategies to write Delphi code that stands the test of time and threat. From safeguarding data to crafting modular architectures and managing legacy, learn how to elevate your codebase while upholding legal and organizational standards.

9.1. Secure Coding Techniques

Injection attacks, buffer overruns, and related security vulnerabilities represent significant risks to Delphi applications, especially those exposed to external inputs or operating in critical environments. Effective mitigation demands a comprehensive approach, combining secure input handling, rigorous validation, and robust error management. These practices help maintain application integrity, prevent unauthorized code execution, and reinforce overall system security.

Injection attacks exploit unchecked or improperly sanitized input to inject malicious code or commands, commonly targeting SQL, shell, or scripting interfaces. In Delphi, SQL injection remains a prevalent concern when dynamic query construction involves user-provided data. To counter this, employing parameterized queries or prepared statements is essential. Parameterization separates code from data, ensuring user inputs do not alter the underlying query structure, as illustrated below:

```
var
  Query: TADOQuery;
begin
  Query := TADOQuery.Create(nil);
  try
    Query.Connection := ADOConnection;
    Query.SQL.Text := 'SELECT * FROM Users WHERE Username = :
    Username';
    Query.Parameters.ParamByName('Username').Value :=
     InputUsername;
    Query.Open;
  finally
    Query.Free;
  end;
end;
```

Here, the use of named parameters (:Username) prevents injection by treating user input strictly as a data value rather than executable SQL code. Avoiding string concatenation of user inputs directly into SQL commands is a foundational rule to prevent injection attacks.

For input handling, comprehensive validation must be enforced both at the client-side and server-side layers, ensuring that inputs conform precisely to expected formats and values before use. Delphi's TryStrToInt, TryStrToDate, and similar functions provide safe conversion mechanisms that prevent exceptions arising from malformed data:

```
var
  UserAge: Integer;
begin
  if not TryStrToInt(UserInputAge, UserAge) then
    raise Exception.Create('Invalid age format.');
end;
```

Validation of length, type, range, and format should be consistently applied to shield applications from a spectrum of issues, including buffer overruns, which occur when a program writes data beyond the allocated memory bounds of a buffer. Buffer overruns can cause unpredictable behavior, crashes, or facilitate the execution of arbitrary code. Delphi's native managed string types reduce such vulnerabilities by enforcing bounds during string operations. However, when working with low-level APIs, arrays, or legacy code in Delphi, careful boundary checking is still crucial.

For example, direct memory manipulation with pointers or manually managed buffers mandates explicit length checks:

```
const
  MaxBufferSize = 256;
var
  Buffer: array[0..MaxBufferSize - 1] of Char;
  InputLen: Integer;
begin
  InputLen := Length(UserInput);
  if InputLen > MaxBufferSize then
    raise Exception.Create('Input exceeds buffer size.');
  Move(PChar(UserInput)^, Buffer, InputLen * SizeOf(Char));
  Buffer[InputLen] := #0; // Null-terminate
end;
```

This snippet guards against buffer overruns by validating input length before copying into a fixed-size buffer. Consistent application of such protective measures prevents potential memory corruption.

Robust error management reinforces secure coding by preventing information leakage and avoiding program crashes that attackers could exploit. Catching exceptions close to the source and logging them securely without exposing sensitive details is a best practice:

```
try
  // Code that might raise an exception
except
  on E: EDatabaseError do
  begin
    LogError('Database operation failed: ' + E.Message);
    ShowMessage('An internal error occurred. Please contact
     support.');
  end;
  on E: Exception do
  begin
    LogError('Unexpected error: ' + E.Message);
    ShowMessage('An unexpected error occurred.');
  end;
end;
```

Here, error messages shown to the user omit technical details to avoid divulging system internals, while logs maintain sufficient information for diagnostics.

Additional practices pertinent to Delphi development include restricting the use of insecure functions, such as those that perform unchecked string copy or format operations (StrCopy, StrCat, Format without argument validation). Prefer safer alternatives like String.Copy, Format with proper control over arguments, and utilize Delphi's UnicodeString type to avoid common pitfalls associated with legacy string types.

Finally, input normalization techniques—such as trimming whitespace, canonicalizing Unicode inputs, and rejecting unexpected characters—mitigate injection vectors and manipulation attempts. Employing comprehensive libraries or writing dedicated sanitization routines calibrated to the application's context further strengthens defense.

In summary, secure coding in Delphi requires a disciplined approach that prioritizes correct handling of user inputs, enforces stringent validation and memory safety, and implements diligent error handling practices. The integration of parameterized queries, safe string operations, and controlled exception management collectively fortifies applications against injection attacks, buffer overruns, and other widespread vulnerabilities.

9.2. Code Organization and Dependency Management

Efficiently structuring large Delphi solutions is paramount for sustaining clarity, maintainability, and scalability over a software project's lifecycle. Central to this goal are the principles of modularization, separation of concerns, and rigorous dependency control. These collectively facilitate a clean architectural design that permits independent development, testing, and evolution of distinct components without cascading impacts.

Delphi's fundamental unit system naturally supports modularization by encapsulating related declarations—types, variables, constants, procedures, and functions—within discrete source files. To maximize this modular advantage in large projects, units should be organized according to coherent functional areas or domain-specific responsibilities. This encourages a "high cohesion, low coupling" design ethos, where each module's internals are focused on a narrow set of related tasks.

Beyond units, Delphi's packages (BPLs) provide an additional modularization layer. Packages allow logical grouping of units into binary modules that can be independently compiled, versioned, and reused across projects. Proper use of packages can significantly reduce compilation times and enable runtime component loading, which is invaluable for plug-in architectures or updating parts of an application without recompiling entirely.

When defining units and packages, one should:

- Ensure clear boundaries between modules by grouping units by feature or service.

- Avoid placing unrelated code within the same unit; instead, create dedicated units to maintain clarity.

- Limit the visibility scope of declarations (interface vs. implementation) to reduce unnecessary exposure and dependency.

Separation of concerns (SoC) is a fundamental architectural guideline that requires distinct features or responsibilities to be handled by discrete components or layers. In Delphi applications, effective use of SoC can be achieved by adopting common architectural patterns such as Model-View-Controller (MVC), Model-View-ViewModel (MVVM), or layered architectures (Presentation, Business Logic, Data Access).

Layers can be realized as sets of units or packages, each responsible for a specific aspect of the application:

- **Presentation Layer:** Handles user interface elements using Forms and Controls. It should have minimal business logic.
- **Business Logic Layer:** Encapsulates domain rules and processes without direct knowledge of UI or data source specifics.
- **Data Access Layer:** Abstracts database and external service communication, providing a consistent API to the business logic layer.

Strictly maintaining layer boundaries ensures that changes within one layer do not ripple unpredictably to others. For instance, business rules can evolve without UI redesign, and database schema modifications can be isolated within the data access units.

Dependencies define how units or packages depend on one another. Poor dependency management can lead to tightly coupled, fragile codebases laden with cyclic references that inhibit maintainability and extensibility.

Delphi units utilize the uses clause to specify dependencies. However, developers must exercise discipline with these clauses to avoid cycles:

- Place reusable and stable units (such as utility, types, or domain model units) early in the dependency graph to avoid frequent recompilations.

- Prefer interface-only uses for dependencies required by the interface section and implementation uses for dependencies needed only in the implementation section to reduce coupling.

- Refactor common dependencies into separate shared units to break cycles.

- Remove uses clauses that are no longer required after refactoring.

In complex projects, cyclic package dependencies are more challenging but crucial to avoid. Delphi's package system enforces acyclic dependency graphs, so one effective strategy is to:

- Extract interfaces and abstractions into dedicated interface packages.

- Implement concrete classes in separate implementation packages that depend on these interfaces.

- Use dependency inversion principles to depend upon abstractions rather than concrete implementations.

This structure not only breaks cycles but introduces extensibility through interface-driven design.

Consider a scenario where a Data Access Layer (DAL) needs to interact with a Business Logic Layer (BLL) without establishing a

221

strong compile-time dependency. Delphi interfaces enable such decoupling by defining contracts that both layers rely on, with implementations provided by the DAL.

```
type
  IDataRepository = interface
    ['{A1B2C3D4-E5F6-7890-1234-56789ABCDEF0}']
    function GetCustomerByID(ID: Integer): TCustomer;
    procedure SaveCustomer(const Customer: TCustomer);
  end;
```

Here, the IDataRepository interface defines methods for customer data operations. The BLL references only this interface, while the DAL provides concrete classes implementing it.

This approach permits injection of different DAL implementations, such as mock repositories for testing or varied database backends, without altering the BLL.

- Adopt strict naming conventions for units and packages to reflect their domain responsibilities clearly.

- Isolate platform-specific or third-party dependencies in dedicated utility units or packages.

- Use package options and conditional compilation directives to manage cross-platform or configuration-specific code.

- Continuously analyze and monitor the dependency graph using Delphi IDE tools or static code analyzers to uncover hidden coupling.

- Document module interfaces and dependency rationale thoroughly to aid team collaboration and future maintenance.

By embracing these practices, developers create Delphi solutions in which each module's role is explicit, dependencies remain well-defined and minimal, and the overall system architecture supports easy evolution. The resulting design reduces technical debt, enhances testability, and accelerates the pace of feature addition and refactoring with confidence.

9.3. Refactoring and Legacy Code Modernization

Refactoring legacy Delphi code demands a systematic and disciplined approach to transform aging codebases into maintainable, extensible, and high-performance systems without altering their external behavior. The objective is to improve code readability, maintainability, and performance to meet modern development standards and business requirements. This section presents an integrated methodology to achieve effective refactoring and modernization of legacy Delphi applications while minimizing risk and effort.

Legacy code is often characterized by monolithic structures, extensive use of global variables, minimal modularization, outdated language constructs, and a lack of adherence to contemporary design principles. These characteristics increase technical debt and reduce the capacity for change and integration with modern platforms such as mobile, cloud, and web ecosystems. The first step in modernization is a comprehensive code assessment using static analysis tools, dependency graphs, and cyclomatic complexity metrics to identify high-risk and high-value refactoring targets. High-complexity modules, tightly coupled components, and frequently modified code areas should be prioritized.

Refactoring should be incremental and iterative, focusing on small, verifiable changes that preserve functionality. Strong version control and continuous integration systems enable frequent commits and automated regression testing, which are crucial for legacy environments lacking full test coverage. Test harnesses must be developed early, including unit, integration, and system tests, to safeguard behavioral equivalence. Code coverage tools can assist in identifying untested parts and guide test creation efforts.

The use of automated refactoring tools tailored for Delphi, such as Castalia or ModelMaker Code Explorer, can expedite the pro-

cess by automating mechanical transformations: renaming identifiers, extracting methods, restructuring inheritance hierarchies,
and detecting dead code. However, many refactoring tasks require
manual intervention, particularly those involving architectural redesign and domain logic improvements.

Key refactoring techniques applicable to legacy Delphi code include:

- **Modularization.** Decompose monolithic units into
  smaller, single-responsibility modules or packages. Delphi's
  unit system facilitates granular separation, allowing
  developers to isolate concerns and improve compilation
  dependencies.

- **Encapsulation.** Replace global variables and public fields
  with well-defined properties and private fields accessed
  through getters and setters, enforcing invariants and
  reducing unintended side effects.

- **Replacing Deprecated Constructs.** Modern Delphi has
  introduced advanced language features like generics, anonymous methods, and attributes. Refactoring legacy code to
  utilize these constructs improves type safety, expressiveness,
  and reduces boilerplate.

- **Eliminating Code Duplication.** Common patterns duplicated across multiple locations should be consolidated into
  reusable functions or classes, improving maintainability and
  reducing error proneness.

- **Improving Naming and Documentation.** Adopt clear,
  consistent naming conventions aligned with contemporary
  standards and include meaningful comments and structured
  documentation to enhance readability.

- **Optimizing Performance.** Profile-guided optimizations
  such as replacing inefficient algorithms, utilizing in-place op-

224

erations, and parallelizing workloads where relevant can substantially improve runtime characteristics without compromising maintainability.

An example illustrating extraction of a complex conditional block into a self-contained method demonstrates these principles:

```
procedure TOrderProcessor.ProcessOrder(Order: TOrder);
begin
  if (Order.Status = osPending) and IsOrderValid(Order) then
  begin
    UpdateOrderStatus(Order, osProcessing);
    try
      ExecuteOrderTransaction(Order);
      UpdateOrderStatus(Order, osCompleted);
    except
      on E: Exception do
      begin
        LogError(E);
        UpdateOrderStatus(Order, osFailed);
        raise;
      end;
    end;
  end;
end;

function TOrderProcessor.IsOrderValid(Order: TOrder): Boolean;
begin
  Result := (Order.Quantity > 0) and (Order.Customer.IsActive);
end;
```

Here, the nested conditions checking order validity are encapsulated in IsOrderValid, isolating business logic from procedural steps, thus improving clarity and enabling targeted unit tests.

Modernizing legacy code also requires addressing obsolete dependencies and interfacing with new technologies. For example, integrating JSON serialization libraries to replace antiquated binary or custom serialization methods is a common improvement. This shift not only simplifies data interchange but also enables interoperability with web services and REST APIs. Delphi's RTL and third-party libraries, such as DelphiMVCFramework or REST.Client, provide abstractions for modern communication protocols, which legacy applications can leverage after refactoring data models accordingly.

Furthermore, shifting from raw pointer management and manual memory handling to managed types and interfaces reduces memory leaks and improves robustness. Refactoring pointer-heavy code to use TList<T>, TDictionary<TKey,TValue>, and interface-based reference counting benefits maintainability and thread safety.

Refactoring approaches must also consider user interface modernization, especially with applications utilizing the outdated VCL visual paradigms. Migrating UI code to FireMonkey (FMX) or adopting responsive designs improves usability and cross-platform reach. This transition often necessitates substantial architectural adjustments, such as decoupling UI logic from business logic using patterns like MVVM (Model-View-ViewModel), which facilitates testability and future evolution.

Risk management during refactoring is critical. Comprehensive impact analysis identifies critical pathways and potential side effects. Employing dependency injection patterns decouples components and simplifies testing and replacement. Additionally, maintaining a robust rollback strategy and documenting all modification rationales improve traceability and knowledge transfer.

Refactoring and modernizing legacy Delphi codebases requires combining automated tooling, disciplined test-driven approaches, modularization strategies, and adoption of modern language and architectural standards. The systematic application of these techniques improves code quality, reduces maintenance costs, and prepares applications for integration within contemporary software ecosystems.

9.4. Documentation and API Design Best Practices

The effective design and maintenance of software systems hinge critically on two intertwined aspects: comprehensive documentation and thoughtfully architected application programming interfaces (APIs). High-quality documentation facilitates developer understanding and adoption, while robust API design ensures longevity, usability, and adaptability to evolving requirements. This section delves into the principles of concise documentation, leverages automated documentation generation tools, and elucidates best practices for crafting stable, user-centered APIs that endure real-world challenges and long-term evolution.

Concise documentation balances brevity and completeness, delivering essential information with minimal verbosity. It avoids redundant explanations while providing sufficient context, examples, and references for efficient comprehension. The primary goal is to reduce cognitive load-developers should spend less time deciphering API intentions and more time leveraging functionalities.

Key elements of effective documentation include:

- *Purpose and Scope*: Clearly state what the API or module accomplishes and its intended use cases.

- *Function Signatures and Parameters*: Enumerate input parameters, return types, side effects, and possible exceptions.

- *Behavioral Details*: Specify preconditions, postconditions, and constraints governing each operation.

- *Examples*: Provide minimal yet illustrative usage patterns that demonstrate typical or recommended workflows.

- *Versioning Notes*: Highlight compatibility guarantees, deprecated features, and migration paths for users.

Conciseness must never undermine completeness; documentation is ideally scoped as "minimum necessary to be useful." For large or complex APIs, modular documentation with well-defined topics and cross-references enhances navigability.

Manual maintenance of extensive documentation is error-prone and resource-intensive. Automated doc-generation tools transform embedded code annotations and structured comments into human-readable documentation, ensuring synchronization between code and descriptive text. Common approaches utilize standardized comment formats such as Javadoc for Java, docstrings in Python, or Doxygen-compatible annotations for multiple languages.

These tools typically support:

- Extraction of metadata from source code annotations.
- Generation of hyperlinked HTML, PDF, or other output formats.
- Inclusion of code examples, inheritance diagrams, and call graphs.
- Custom styling and templating for brand or project-specific appearances.

An example of a typical annotation for a function in a C++ project using Doxygen syntax is:

```
/**
 * Calculates the square root of a non-negative value.
 *
 * @param x the input value, must be non-negative
 * @return the square root of x
 * @throws std::domain_error if x is negative
 */
double sqrt_safe(double x);
```

Running Doxygen on such annotated code generates browsable HTML documentation with clear function descriptions, parameter lists, and exception behaviors linked directly to the source code.

Integrating automated documentation generation into continuous integration pipelines promotes up-to-date, accurate documentation and reinforces best practices in code commenting.

API longevity and usability require deliberate design decisions that anticipate future enhancements and diverse user requirements. The following best practices are broadly recognized within advanced software engineering disciplines:

Design for Compatibility and Versioning

Introduce semantic versioning to communicate breaking and non-breaking changes clearly. Maintain backward compatibility whenever possible; if breaking changes are inevitable, provide clear migration paths. For example, utilize deprecation warnings and phased removals to minimize user disruption.

Principle of Least Surprise

APIs should behave in ways intuitive to experienced users-naming conventions, parameter ordering, default behaviors, and error handling must align with common expectations within the language or domain ecosystem.

Explicit and Predictable Behavior

Clearly define the contracts for each function or endpoint. Avoid implicit side effects and hidden state changes, which complicate debugging and testing. The following table summarizes important contract attributes:

Contract Attribute	Description
Preconditions	Conditions that must hold before invocation (e.g., non-null parameters).
Postconditions	Guarantees after execution (e.g., returned values or state changes).
Invariants	Internal state conditions maintained throughout API usage.
Exceptions	Types of errors that can be thrown and under which conditions.

Minimal Surface Area

Expose only necessary components to reduce cognitive load and attack surface. Encapsulate internal mechanisms and avoid leaking implementation details. Favor composition and extension mechanisms over monolithic interfaces.

Consistency Across the API

Consistency in naming, parameter ordering, error codes, and data representations improves learnability and reduces user errors. Establish style guides and automated linters where feasible.

Granularity and Modularity

APIs should present coherent units of functionality without overwhelming the user. Modularize logically to allow users to adopt subsets as needed, fostering flexible integration.

Documentation as Part of the API

Design APIs with self-documenting elements such as descriptive identifiers and embedded metadata, enabling runtime inspection or help commands where applicable.

Consider an API endpoint that retrieves user information. An initial design exposing a generous set of fields might later necessitate restricting returned data for privacy compliance. A stable API anticipates extension by versioning the endpoint or allowing optional fields selected via query parameters rather than removing fields outright.

Similarly, when evolving authentication mechanisms, providing both legacy and modern token schemes during a transition phase preserves client compatibility and allows incremental upgrades.

The confluence of well-maintained documentation and resilient API design generates a virtuous cycle: clear documentation reduces misuse and support demands, while stable, intuitive APIs foster user confidence and straightforward documentation. Automated tools bridge the gap between source code and external text, minimizing divergence and maintenance overhead. Consistent adherence to well-established principles contributes to software assets that serve both immediate implementation and sustained evolution objectives.

9.5. Design Patterns Revisited in Delphi

In the context of Delphi programming, design patterns assume a particular character shaped by the language's native constructs, the VCL framework, and the evolving paradigms of contemporary software development. Revisiting classic design patterns with a Delphi lens reveals opportunities for adaptation and evolution that are crucial for maintainability and scalability in modern applications.

The *Singleton* pattern, traditionally enforcing a single instance of a class, finds straightforward implementation in Delphi through the use of a class variable scoped to the unit. However, Delphi's support for thread-safe initialization since Delphi 2009 introduces a refined idiom using the `TMonitor` or `TCriticalSection` to handle concurrency concerns. For example:

```
type
  TConfiguration = class
  private
    class var FInstance: TConfiguration;
    class var FLock: TObject;
  public
    class function GetInstance: TConfiguration;
  end;

class function TConfiguration.GetInstance: TConfiguration;
begin
  if FInstance = nil then
  begin
    TMonitor.Enter(FLock);
    try
      if FInstance = nil then
        FInstance := TConfiguration.Create;
    finally
      TMonitor.Exit(FLock);
    end;
  end;
  Result := FInstance;
end;
```

This adaptation protects against multi-threaded initialization races, a necessity in contemporary multi-core environments. Leveraging class var fields and Delphi's managed interface reference counting for lifecycle management further enhances robustness.

Transitioning to the *Observer* pattern, Delphi's native TNotifyEvent and event delegation mechanisms offer an idiomatic approach. Unlike classical observer implementations mandating explicit subject and observer interfaces, Delphi's event model centralizes event subscription and notification through method pointers. The pattern morphs into a more succinct, loosely coupled event-driven design:

```
type
  TSubject = class
  private
    FOnChange: TNotifyEvent;
  public
    procedure Attach(AObserver: TNotifyEvent);
    procedure Detach(AObserver: TNotifyEvent);
    procedure Notify;
    property OnChange: TNotifyEvent read FOnChange write
      FOnChange;
  end;

procedure TSubject.Attach(AObserver: TNotifyEvent);
begin
  FOnChange := TNotifyEvent.Combine(FOnChange, AObserver);
end;

procedure TSubject.Detach(AObserver: TNotifyEvent);
begin
  FOnChange := TNotifyEvent.Remove(FOnChange, AObserver);
end;

procedure TSubject.Notify;
begin
  if Assigned(FOnChange) then
    FOnChange(Self);
end;
```

This idiom illustrates how the tight coupling between subject and observers is mitigated using Delphi's native multicast delegates, fostering decoupled, maintainable components.

The *Factory* pattern experiences a noteworthy evolution with Delphi's extended support for generics and anonymous methods. Factories can be abstracted into generic classes or records, supplying type-safe instance creation encapsulated in functions passed as parameters. This approach aligns the classical creational pattern with modern language capabilities, as demonstrated below:

```
type
  TFactory<T: class> = record
  private
    FCreator: TFunc<T>;
  public
    constructor Create(ACreator: TFunc<T>);
    function CreateInstance: T;
  end;

constructor TFactory<T>.Create(ACreator: TFunc<T>);
begin
  FCreator := ACreator;
end;

function TFactory<T>.CreateInstance: T;
begin
  Result := FCreator();
end;
```

The above generic factory promotes extensibility by allowing client code to specify creation logic dynamically. It also harmonizes well with dependency injection frameworks, enabling inversion of control principles in Delphi applications.

The *Decorator* pattern, aimed at augmenting object behavior dynamically, is often implemented in Delphi by leveraging interface inheritance coupled with reference counting to manage lifetimes. Interfaces provide a flexible contract model, allowing decorators to wrap original objects transparently. Consider an interface-driven decorator pattern:

```
type
  IComponent = interface
    ['{8A0F0B72-2C4A-42D1-9B2E-ACF0E59F48E1}']
    procedure Operation;
  end;

  TConcreteComponent = class(TInterfacedObject, IComponent)
  public
    procedure Operation;
  end;

  TDecorator = class(TInterfacedObject, IComponent)
```

233

```
private
  FComponent: IComponent;
public
  constructor Create(AComponent: IComponent);
  procedure Operation; virtual;
end;

procedure TConcreteComponent.Operation;
begin
  // Core behavior implemented here
end;

constructor TDecorator.Create(AComponent: IComponent);
begin
  inherited Create;
  FComponent := AComponent;
end;

procedure TDecorator.Operation;
begin
  FComponent.Operation;
  // Additional behavior here
end;
```

This pattern's flexibility is particularly suited to the dynamic runtime modification requirements of contemporary GUI components or middleware layers in Delphi.

Recent trends in software architecture encourage the *Repository* pattern to abstract data access, decoupling domain logic from persistence mechanisms. Delphi's strong typing and interface support enable comprehensive repository implementations that also accommodate asynchronous operations using the IAsyncResult pattern or parallel programming libraries (System.Threading). By defining repositories through interfaces, one achieves testable, replaceable components:

```
type
  IEntity = interface
    ['{3560E3B7-1B7F-4C39-9E3F-0676AF11FCFE}']
    function GetID: Integer;
  end;

  IRepository<T: IEntity> = interface
    ['{A5679E9D-2FCF-4B8B-9502-E34806E47496}']
    function Add(const Entity: T): Boolean;
    function Remove(const Entity: T): Boolean;
```

```
    function FindByID(ID: Integer): T;
end;
```

Integration of this pattern with ORM frameworks such as Delphi's FireDAC or third-party solutions improves maintainability by segregating data concerns cleanly.

Emerging design patterns tailor-made for modern Delphi development extend beyond traditional creational, structural, and behavioral categories. The *Mediator* pattern, for example, facilitates interaction management between multiple components, reducing coupling complexity in event-driven environments or multithreaded applications. Delphi's RTL and component framework support this with message dispatchers and centralized event buses, often implemented as singleton service locators for system-wide coordination.

Moreover, the rise of reactive programming paradigms encourages the adoption of patterns such as the *Observer* in reactive streams or signals/slots analogues in Delphi's LiveBindings framework. This leverages Delphi's reflective RTTI to bind UI controls dynamically to data sources with minimal boilerplate, promoting declarative, maintainable interfaces aligned with MVVM or MVP architectures.

Together, these adaptations and innovations underscore the continued relevance of design patterns in Delphi, emphasizing evolution to harness language-specific features while addressing current demands of application scalability, testability, and concurrency. By grounding classical principles within Delphi's evolving ecosystem, developers ensure robust, extensible software that capitalizes on both historical wisdom and modern practicality.

9.6. Legal, Licensing, and Compliance Considerations

When integrating third-party Delphi code-whether open-source or proprietary-into software projects, understanding the legal and licensing frameworks governing such use is indispensable. The ramifications of non-compliance extend beyond financial liabilities, potentially causing reputational damage and jeopardizing the project's sustainability. This section elucidates the core legal obligations, licensing typologies, and compliance strategies pertinent to Delphi development environments, emphasizing responsible and sustainable software practices.

Open-source licensing operates under various paradigms, with licenses ranging from permissive to restrictive. Permissive licenses, such as the MIT License and the BSD family, impose minimal conditions on reuse, typically requiring only attribution to the original authors. In contrast, copyleft licenses like the GNU General Public License (GPL) and its variant, the GNU Affero General Public License (AGPL), mandate that derivative works also be distributed under the same license terms. In Delphi development, the choice of incorporating open-source components governed by copyleft licenses necessitates careful consideration, as it may compel the entire application to be open-sourced, potentially conflicting with proprietary business models.

Proprietary code licenses, often characterized by vendor-specific agreements, customarily restrict redistribution and modification. These licenses may be perpetual or subscription-based and frequently include clauses prescribing limitations on usage, reverse engineering, and sublicensing. When engaging with proprietary Delphi libraries or tools, thorough vetting of license agreements is mandatory to align the project's scope with legal constraints. Ignorance of such terms can lead to onerous breach of contract claims or revocation of usage rights.

Compliance frameworks extend beyond license adherence to encompass regulatory mandates, particularly when software handles sensitive data or operates in regulated industries. Standards such as the General Data Protection Regulation (GDPR) in the European Union or the Health Insurance Portability and Accountability Act (HIPAA) in the United States impose requirements on data privacy, security, and auditability. Delphi developers must ensure that integrated code, including third-party components, does not introduce vulnerabilities or non-compliant data practices. This involves conducting code audits, penetration testing, and maintaining clear documentation of data flows, especially when components utilize external APIs or services.

A proactive approach to legal and licensing compliance in Delphi projects involves implementing a Software Bill of Materials (SBOM). An SBOM catalogs all third-party components, their licenses, and versioning details, serving as an essential artifact for compliance verification and vulnerability management. Consider the following snippet illustrating a simplified SBOM representation in JSON format for Delphi project dependencies:

```json
{
  "components": [
    {
      "name": "Delphi VCL",
      "version": "10.4",
      "license": "Proprietary"
    },
    {
      "name": "Indy Components",
      "version": "10.6.2",
      "license": "BSD-3-Clause"
    },
    {
      "name": "Synopse mORMot",
      "version": "1.18",
      "license": "MPL-1.1"
    }
  ]
}
```

Maintaining an accurate SBOM facilitates the identification of license conflicts and supports rapid response to disclosed vulnerabilities in dependencies. Continuous integration pipelines can integrate automated SBOM generation and license scanning tools to reinforce compliance rigor throughout the development lifecycle.

In addition to license and regulatory compliance, ethical considerations form a growing dimension of responsible software development. Sustainable software practices encompass respecting user privacy, ensuring accessibility, and fostering transparency regarding embedded third-party code. Developers are encouraged to adopt License Compatibility Matrices and develop internal policies that document permissible licenses and their implications on deliverables. Such matrices enable deterministic decision-making and reduce inadvertent violations stemming from ambiguous license terms.

Automated tools tailored for Delphi projects have matured to aid compliance efforts. Static analysis tools can flag potential license conflicts by scanning source files and package manifests. For instance, integrating tools like FOSSA or Black Duck through command-line interfaces within build scripts allows compliance teams to generate comprehensive audit reports without disrupting developer workflows. These reports highlight high-risk licenses and expose unauthorized code usage, enabling informed remediation before release.

From a contractual perspective, organizations should negotiate indemnification clauses and warranties with licensors, especially for proprietary components, to mitigate legal exposure arising from code defects or intellectual property infringements. It is prudent to maintain clear, written agreements delineating distribution rights, support obligations, and update policies.

Ultimately, achieving sustainable compliance with legal and licensing obligations in Delphi development necessitates a multi-faceted strategy incorporating education, tooling, process integration, and organizational policies. The cohesive alignment of legal awareness, technical safeguards, and ethical responsibility fosters software products that are not only robust and functional but also legally sound and respected within the technology ecosystem.

www.ingramcontent.com/pod-product-compliance
Lightning Source LLC
Chambersburg PA
CBHW061244220326
41599CB00028B/5531